Jewish Ritual Washing

and

Christian Baptism:

Evolution or Revolution?

Jewish Ritual Washing
and
Christian Baptism:
Evolution or Revolution?

William H. Jones

ChiRho Communications

[wmhjones9@gmail.com]

Toronto

ISBN 978-0-929081-20-5

Jewish Ritual Washing and Christian Baptism: Evolution or Revolution?
By William H. Jones. All rights reserved.
Copyright © 2010 [wmhjones9@gmail.com]
Cover photo by William H. Jones shows a *mikveh* at Masada, the first uncovered in modern Israel.

Acknowledgments:

Appreciation is herewith expressed to Dr. Richard N. Longenecker, who allowed me to produce an M.Th. thesis on this subject at McMaster Divinity College / University, and to two thesis readers and oral examiners, Dr. Michael Knowles of the Divinity College and Dr. Eileen Schuller, of McMaster's Department of Religion.

Appreciation is also expressed to my pastor, Rev. Dr. John A. Forrester, who encouraged me to update the thesis and put it in book form.

Contents

Chapter 6

Introduction

During the years of Jesus' life on earth, part of which coincided with the Qumranite history, ritual immersion was an entrenched part of Jewish efforts to achieve ritual purity.[1] Hartmut Stegemann states that ritual immersion in the *mikve'ot* was a common rite "in the Judaism of the time, which the Essenes only practised more than did other Jews."[2]

No worshipper to the Temple could enter its precincts without first immersing himself in the *mikveh*. Ritual cleansing was a prerequisite to Temple worship.[3] The male worshippers first ritually purified themselves in the immersion vat, then climbed to the Temple Mount through the three doors of the eastern Hulda Gates. Priests and Levites used different *mikve'ot* near a separate entrance. Likewise, women used a separate *mikveh* to enter the Women's Court. The Ophel's director of archaeology, Professor Meir Ben-Dov, was surprised by the number of *mikve'ot* he unearthed within private homes. He speculated that home owners rented their premises to pilgrims who wanted a lodging adjacent to the Temple.

---

[1] Lawrence H. Schiffman. Reclaiming the Dead Sea Scrolls. New York: Doubleday, 1995. p. 403.

[2] Hartmut Stegemann. The Library of Qumran. Grand Rapids MI: William B. Eerdmans Publishing Company, 1998. p. 222.

[3] Meier Ben-Dov. In the Shadow of the Temple. Jerusalem: Keter Publishing House, 1985. p. 153.

He pondered if the pilgrims to Jerusalem on festival days, saw room-for-rent signs that invited them to lease a temporary private space which included a *mikveh*. "That is how I would explain the profusion of these baths, for many of the householders living near the Temple Mount made a living from renting out rooms."[4]

The existence and extent of these ritual baths raise important questions about their connection to Christian baptism. How is the practice of the *mikveh* connected to John's baptism? When Jesus or his disciples entered the Temple Mount did they also immerse themselves ritually? Why, in New Testament Christian practice, does an agent get involved in the baptism whereas in the *mikveh*, the worshipper immersed himself? Were women also part of the *mikveh* ritual?

Archaeological discoveries at the Ophel, the southern entrance area to the Temple Mount in Jerusalem, beg deeper investigation into the relationship of Jewish immersion practices (*tevilah*) and Christian baptism. The discovery of so many ritual baths (*mikve'ot*) has unveiled for Christians what may be a neglected study of the Jewish practice of ritual immersion. How does it relate to Christian baptism? This book will explore those rites, both those connected to worship at the Temple Mount and in private homes or in places of prayer. It will also examine the development of Christian baptism.

In a 1981 private interview with Matty Zohar, an archaeologist working *in situ* at the Ophel, this writer learned from him that to that date, cisterns with the capacity of nine million cubic metres dotted the slopes of the Ophel to provide water for the *mikve'ot*. These cisterns were fed from

---

[4] Ibid.

both rainwater, some seepage and an aqueduct built by Herod's engineers, so that water could flow from sources near Bethlehem to supply all of Jerusalem's ritualistic needs.

In 1982, Meir Ben Dov, the chief archaeologist for the Temple Mount area, indicated that to that date 48 *mikve'ot* had been excavated.[5] In June, 2010, this writer asked Professor Dan Bahat, the distinguished former city archaeologist of Jerusalem, if more had been found. By email he replied, "I can add, after my excavations in the Western Wall, Tunnel three (3) more and very special ones. Professor (Ronny) Reich[6] has identified two *miqves* on the Temple Mount proper. The more we dig, the more we find."

Each *mikveh* was accompanied by a reservoir beside it. A "legitimate" *mikveh* needed to hold a minimum of 40 *seah* (var. *se'ah*) or approximately 800 litres of "ritually clean water" to feed and ensure that water in the *mikveh* (var. *mikve, mikvah, miqwa*)) was ritually purified. The formula for ritual purification was proscribed by the religious precepts of the *halaka(h)*, the Jewish code of correct conduct.

This book searches for answers to some of these issues and explores both the similarities and the differences between the ritual baths of the "Second Temple" as well as the Qumranites, and the developing practices, first of John the Baptist, and then of the earliest Christian baptisms.

---

[5] Meier Ben-Dov. op. cit., p152

[6] Ronny Reich 's 1990 Ph.D. dissertation, Miqwa'ot (Jewish Ritual Baths) in Eretz-Izrael, in the Second Temple and Talmud Periods, was supervised by Professors Nahman Avigad and I. L. Levine.

1. The *Mikveh* Ritual

Soon after the Dead Sea Scrolls were discovered in 1947 at Caves I, then later at IV and V at Qumran, excavators found corroborating documents and archaeological remains which revealed the daily immersion practices of the Qumran Community. They were further corroborated by the previously known writings of Josephus. This separatist religious community of Essenes rejected the Temple practices, in part, because they thought the priesthood was corrupt.

Thus the Essenes at Qumran developed an *ad hoc* theology which allowed them to avoid the sacrificial nature of Temple worship, while maintaining some of the ritual practices which accompanied Temple worship.[7]

One of these maintained rituals was self-immersion. Excavators at Qumran uncovered the remnants of both cisterns and *mikve'ot*. Evidently, the Essenes continued to wash themselves ritually almost as if the Temple was a part of their community life. Indeed, they outdid the immersions performed by other Jews elsewhere.

Their immersions were a daily regimen. In a way, their practising of immersions and their communal meals bore some similarities to Christian baptism and communion. Yigael Yadin[8] speculated that if John the Baptist was not actually a part of this Qumran Community, he certainly knew about the Essenes' daily rituals. Likely, his baptismal ministry was somehow remotely connected to that group.

---

[7] Personal interview on videotape with Professor Yigael Yadin, November 1981 at the Shrine of the Book in Jerusalem.

[8] Ibid.

12

More *mikve'ot* have been uncovered elsewhere in Israel. In the Jewish Quarter of Jerusalem, a grand mansion[9] was excavated which showed a *mikveh* within the house, adjacent to the Temple Mount.

Several *mikve'ot* were unearthed in the former Essene Quarter of Jerusalem.[10] One was found in what is now St. Joseph's Roman Catholic Church in Nazareth. At the Herodium and at Masada,[11] *mikve'ot* were unearthed near synagogues. Professor Reich has discovered many more *mikve'ot* at excavations at Sepphoris in Galilee.

Mikve'ot were human-dug pits created to simulate a stream, with "pure" water flowing from a "pure" source by way of a small hole or channel, usually stoppered until more water was needed in the *mikveh*. Then it was opened so that the "treasury" or "purified" cistern could fill any lack of adequate water in the immersion vat. In nature, rivers were ideal for ritual cleansings.[12] Various aspects of ritual immersion are further examined.

---

[9] Nahman Avigad. Discovering Jerusalem, p. 142.

[10] James H. Charlesworth. (ed.). Jesus and the Dead Sea Scrolls. New York: Doubleday, 1992, 1995. p. 329.

[11] Yigael Yadin. Masada: Herod's Fortress and the Zealot's Last Stand. Great Britain: George Weidenfeld & Nicholson Limited, 1966, 1984. , p. 165-7.

[12] Acts 16:13

2. *Mikveh* Connections with Jesus and His Disciples

This book looks at some possible connections with the *mikveh* in Jesus' words and in his disciples' practices. For example, what did Jesus mean when he said, "Unless one is born of water and the Spirit he cannot enter the kingdom of God?"[13] Was this a reference to the ritual washing which Nicodemus would regularly undergo as an obedient Pharisee? Or, did it refer to the amnionic waters of human birth? Or, was Jesus referring to both?

What about the baptisms conducted by John the Baptist or in the name of John?[14] How are these linked, if at all, to Jewish ritual immersion? What is the meaning of Jesus' Upper Room comment to Peter about his "having bathed?"[15] What does it mean that Jesus' disciples baptized but he did not?[16] How do we interpret Jesus' commission to followers to scatter throughout the world to "disciple-ize" humanity and in so doing, baptize everyone in the name of the Trinity while instructing them about the kingdom of God?[17]

3. Agents and Frequency in Baptism

This book examines what appears to be much different purposes between Jewish ritual immersion and Christian

---

[13] John 3:5

[14] Acts 19:1-7

[15] John 13:10

[16] John 4:1, 2

[17] Matthew 28:19, 20

baptism. Jewish ritual immersion appears, by definition, to be "a ritual," and is frequently repeated. Christian baptism appears to be a "one-time" initiation activity. Jewish ritual immersion appears to be self-activated. Christian baptism seems to imply an agent in the conducting of baptism. This book will examine these factors to see if there are exceptions to these generalizations.

4. Christian Baptism: Its Purpose, Meaning and Requirements

What is the purpose of baptism? What were the reasons Jesus submitted to baptism? Is it essential for discipleship in God's kingdom? If so, why do Quakers not follow Jesus' instructions to baptize believers? Why does John Stott, an evangelical clergyperson in the Anglican communion, raise questions about baptism (and communion) as nonessentials (*adiaphora*, "matters indifferent") which only hinder the co-operative ministry of all evangelicals?[18]

Is baptism a symbol of something larger? How is baptism connected to initiation into the new believer's life? Is the proselyte baptism required in conversion to Judaism, a covenantal form of initiation rite essential to a new Christian? How does baptism reflect the death and resurrection of Jesus? Are elements of these symbols evident in the ritual immersion practices of the *mikveh*? Is baptism a means of God's grace? Is it a covenantal link with God? Once administered, should baptism be re-administered?

---

[18] John Stott. Evangelical Truth, pp. 176,177.

15

Summary

Clearly, Christian baptism did not appear suddenly without similar precedents in Judaism. Indeed, forms of baptism may be seen in non-monotheistic religions as well. According to Euripides, at Delphi, in Greece, priests, temple officials and pilgrims cleansed themselves at the Castilia spring as part of the worship of Apollo.[19]

Earlier influences such as pilgrim baptisms among pagan religions may have had a part in setting the stage for the water cleansing associated with Christian baptism. George R. Beasley-Murray points out that ancient peoples found mystery in water and insinuated that water held divine properties. The progression from water as special and sacred to water used ritualistically was an easy advance. Bathing in "special" water reflected homage to the spirits indwelling the waters. Consequently, water became a blessing, a protection from evil and a symbol of healing.[20]

The Jewish practice of the *mikveh*, however, may more closely resemble the genesis of Christian baptism than any pagan rites. How similar and how dissimilar, how dependent and how separate are the two, is the subject of the following chapters.

---

[19] Basil Petrakos. Delphi, p. 35.

[20] G. R. Beasley-Murray. Baptism in the New Testament. Grand Rapids MI: William B. Eerdmans Publishing Company, 1962, 1994. pp. 3, 4.

16

Part One: Jewish Ritual Washing

CHAPTER 1

The Response of a Good Conscience toward God

Water is a cleansing agent. Clean water helps to purify our bodies. When we bathe, we not only remove the grime and impurities from our skin, we "feel better" for it. Water, therefore, is an important symbol of inner purity. Bathing for spiritual purposes signifies a sense of purity within and thereby enhances our sensitivity to spiritual influences.

Religious groups have long recognized water as a symbol of purification. At what Hindus consider "the Holy City" of Varanasi (Benares) in India, the pilgrims descend their pilgrim steps and wade into the Ganges to immerse themselves as part of their personal spiritual renewal. Although the river is ecologically damaged and the water is severely polluted, the symbolism of spiritual cleansing is more powerful to them than the reality.

1. Washings and Cleansings in the Old Testament

a. Biblical References to Walking with God

From the beginning of their intertwined relationship God challenged his chosen people to walk closely with him. To Moses, God said, "I will test them and see whether they will follow my instructions"(NIV).[21] The translation more literally may read, *"to see if they will walk in my torah or*

---

[21] Exodus 16:4.

not."[22] When appraising the sons / judges whom Samuel had appointed, the elders recognized that *halaka* was not a part of their commitment to God as Samuel's had been. "Your sons do not walk in your ways; now appoint a king to lead us . . ."[23]

Sensitive Israelites did, however, seek to walk with God. They considered it no detrimental obligation but a delight and privilege. Although his path may take him through the "valley of the shadow of death," the poet of Psalm 23 understood that he could walk there knowing that the LORD walked with him.

The opening psalm of the psalter speaks of both negative and positive results from walking. Obviously, walking with God (*halaka*) is the best choice. It results in fruitfulness and prosperity. Walking with the wicked, sinners or mockers leads to immobility and paralysis.

> Blessed is the man
> who does not walk in the counsel of the wicked
>> or stand in the way of sinners or sit in the seat of
> mockers.
> But his delight is in the law of the LORD,
>> and on his law he mediates day and night.
> He is like a tree planted by streams of water,
>> which yields its fruit in season
>> and whose leaf does not wither. Whatever he does
> prospers.
>> Not so the wicked! They are like chaff that the wind
> blows away.
> Therefore the wicked will not stand in the judgment,
>> nor sinners in the assembly of the righteous.

---

[22] Roy L. Honeycutt Jr., The Broadman Bible Commentary Volume 1: Exodus (original publication), p. 397.

[23] 1 Samuel 8:5.

For the LORD watches over the way of the righteous,
but the way of the wicked will perish.[24]

Eugene Peterson's paraphrase of Psalm 119 hints at the joy some of God's people found in letting God set the parameters of their lives by his clear guidance:

I watch my step, avoiding the ditches and ruts of evil
so I can spend all my time keeping your Word.
I never make detours from the route you laid out;
you gave me such good directions.
Your words are so choice, so tasty;
I prefer them to home cooking . . .
By your words I can see where I am going;
they throw a beam of light on my dark path.
I've committed myself and I'll never turn back
from living by your righteous order . . .

The prophets constantly called Israel to espouse *halaka*. Isaiah spoke of walking with the LORD throughout his prophecies. One instance will suffice to stress this emphasis;

If you keep your feet from breaking the Sabbath and from doing what you please on my holy day, if you call the Sabbath a delight and the LORD's holy day honourable, and if you honour it by not going your own way and not doing as you please or speaking idle words, then you will find your joy in the LORD, and I will cause you to ride on the heights of the land and to feast on the inheritance of your father Jacob."[25]

Note the reference to "feet" and "walking" and contrast

---

[24] Psalm 1.

[25] Isaiah 58:13, 14.

the present tiring work of walking with the end divine reward of riding and feasting. In other words, the present roots put down by holy disciplines will later translate into fabulous future fruit. Jeremiah follows with a similar observation: "Stand at the crossroads and look; ask for the ancient paths, and ask where the good way is, and walk in it and you will find rest for your souls."[26]

Isaiah tells of the righteous teacher whose life will be visible and whose guiding, sanctifying word will be clearly audible. "He who is your teacher will hide no longer, and you will see your teacher with your own eyes. Whether you turn to the right or left, your ears will hear these words behind you, 'This is the way, follow it.'"[27]

The Rabbinic "spin" on walking with the LORD evolved from Temple precedents to what Rabbi Stuart Rosenberg described as a "warm and loving feeling for humanity into the daily habit every Jew by means of the *halaka*."[28] This "walk" was redefined after the Temple was destroyed and Rabbinical Judaism was born and flourished.

> The *halaka* of the Rabbis reshaped prophetism and gave its lofty, humane concerns a concrete order and structure. Every commonplace, daily human habit could become sacred – as the Rabbis insisted it should be seen – as an act of worship. The loving deed became more important than the cult of the Temple.[29]

---

[26] Jeremiah 6:16.

[27] Isaiah 30: 20, 21.

[28] Stuart Rosenberg. To Understand Jews, p. 40.

[29] Stuart Rosenberg. op. cit., p. 41.

b. Ritual Washing

The Bible is replete with references to "a gathering of waters" as well as to the practice of ceremonial washing. The Bible also relates situations in which the matter of uncleanness is implied, if not explicit. For example, one reads the Genesis story of Rachael deceiving her father Laban concerning her theft of his household gods (*terephim*). He searched everywhere in her tent for them but could not find them. She had hidden them in the saddlebags on her camel and was sitting on them. Rachel knew her father could not touch the saddle or its covering because she had a menstrual flow.

For him to touch even her saddle would make him unclean, with all the implications of inconvenience that would cause him. "Don't be angry, my Lord, that I cannot stand up in your presence; I'm having my period' So he searched but could not find the household gods."[30] Laban would have needed to bathe himself, wash his garments and be in isolation until he was "ritually clean." The irony of the situation is compounded by Rachael's making the *terephim* unclean and therefore invalid for being efficacious.

Even prior to the *halaka* being codified, before Rachael's obvious understanding of the requirements of being "ritually clean," the unwritten rules of *halaka* were clearly understood. Leviticus states the order precisely: "When a woman has her regular flow of blood, the impurity of her monthly period will last seven days and anyone who touches her will be unclean until evening . . . anything she lies on during her period will be unclean and anything she sits on will be unclean . . . whoever touches anything she sits

---

[30] Genesis 31:35.

23

on must wash his clothes and bathe with water."[31]

The symbolism of being born from the water is implied in the story of Moses' redemption from the papyrus ark floating on the Nile River. His name, Moishe, means "out of the water" and combines the Egyptian names of pharaohs with the sense that he was the pathfinder of the Hebrew and future Jewish people who also would rise from water into the affection and pleasure of the LORD.

In this story, the daughter of the pharaoh came to the river to wash herself. Are the writers of Exodus telling their readers that hers was a ritual bath in a "collection of waters?" The birth story of Moses and his salvation from the Nile has an interesting parallel using similar words in the birth story of Sargon of Agarde. [32]

The operative word for ritual washing is immersion. The *Torah* taught that a person "shall wash all his flesh in the water."[33] The Hebrew word *rachatz* means "to wash" but it also means "to purify with water."[34] When Naaman was told by Elisha to wash in the Jordan, the prophet used the word *rachatz,* "to wash." The Bible states that he then went down and immersed (*taval*) himself in the Jordan."[35] "To wash," therefore, sometimes was understood to mean "to immerse." Interestingly, the Septuagint (LXX) translates Naaman's

---

[31] Leviticus 15:19–23.

[32] J. Coert Rylaarsdam. The Book of Exodus, The Interpreter's Bible Vol. 1., p. 859.

[33] Leviticus 15:16.

[34] Aryeh Kaplan. Waters of Eden, p. 7.

[35] 2 Kings 5:10; Aryeh Kaplan. op. cit., p. 58.

immersion in the Jordan River, using the Greek word, *baptizo*. *Baptizo* translates dip, plunge, submerse or immerse.[36]

2. Ritual Bathing in Early and Rabbinic Judaism

a. *Halaka* or Walking with God

Jews,[37] like many Greeks, Romans and Asian peoples, also practised ritual washing (*tevilah*). Perhaps the imperative of *tevilah* took on special, urgent meaning because its frequent usage helped Jews maintain their unique Jewishness in the face of subtle, ubiquitous, pervasive Hellenistic and Roman cultures. The washings were set in traditions firmly grounded in a sense of divine leading which Jews call *halaka (var. halakha, halakhah)*. *Halaka* means "walking," "walking with God." The descriptive word derived from Rabbinical Judaism after the destruction of Jerusalem in AD 70 although the *Oral Torah* traditions supported ritual washing even before the rabbis codified *halaka*.

The religious leadership of Jerusalem in the Hellenistic period first consisted of priests, followed by elders – *gerousia*. Evidently, another ruling institution developed more or less about the time of Jesus. It was known as the *Sanhedrin*. It was a tribunal and political institution.

---

[36] Herschel H. Hobbs. The Baptist Faith and Message. p. 84.

[37] The term "Jew" or "Jewish" is used in this document in a generic sense to mean all the tribes of Israel. Paul spoke of "we Jews" (Galatians 2:15) and yet he was of the tribe of Benjamin (Philippians 3:5).

Apparently, the high priest was a member of it. But, as Michael's Stone's edited work points out, "The rabbinic sources . . . frequently refer to the *Sanhedrin* (or the Great Court) . . . as a legislative body comprised of 70 or 71 elders, 'from whence *halakhah* goes out to Israel.'"[38] Thus, even before the Jamnia conference about AD 100 which instituted Rabbinic Judaism following the destruction of Jerusalem, the system of *halaka* was at the core of Jewish existence.

"*Halaka* is walking in the 'way of the LORD,'" wrote Rabbi Stuart Rosenberg. "What the priests had made into the cold and impersonal commands of the Scripture, Rabbinic *halaka* clothed with warmth of a new zeal: to build God's kingdom on earth by learning to do his will within the human situation."[39] *Halaka* is symbolic of a return to an Eden in which humankind can walk shamelessly in the garden with the LORD God.[40] Humanity seems to have an innate desire to re-discover Eden.

"*The way of the LORD*" was a phrase known long before the rabbis codified it. When Deutero-Isaiah opened his prophecy in the 40th chapter of Isaiah, he used the term (the way of the LORD) as a prophecy of hope for the exiled Jews. Indeed, while Jews were unavoidably absent from Jerusalem during those years in Babylonia, their customs, regulations and daily religious rituals were their means of ethnic identity and solidarity.

Later, when Christians suffered persecution at the hands of Jerusalem's religious elite, the fledgling Christian

---

[38] Michael Stone, ed. <u>Jewish Writings of the Second Temple Period</u>, p. 23.

[39] Stuart Rosenberg. <u>To Understand Jews</u>, p. 40.

[40] Genesis 3:8.

believers became identified as "the Way."[41] In part they took this cue from Jesus who told his disciples he was "the way, the truth and the life."[42] In that statement, did not Jesus imply that walking with him was the same thing as *halaka*? Certainly, the reference to "walking with" Jesus Christ is scattered throughout the New Testament.[43]

John the Baptist's ministry as herald of Messiah perhaps had a *double entendre* in that he was preparing "the way for the LORD" and "making straight the crooked places."[44] John was also preparing for a new *halaka*, a new way to walk with God. Later Jesus said, "no one comes to the Father except through me."[45] One interpretation of that may be that Jesus is the ultimate *halaka* in which the fulness of God is to be found.

Not all Jews practised solidarity in keeping the spirit and the letter of *halaka*. About one-third of the Babylonian Talmud is about *halaka*. The remainder comprises parables and stories.[46] As Julian Obermann wrote in his foreword to Danby's translation of the *Book of Cleanness*, [Maimonides' *Mishnah Torah*] "Except that he might not enter the Temple of Jerusalem (when it was in existence) or eat of 'hallowed'

---

[41] Acts 2:9.

[42] John 14:6.

[43] John 12:35; Romans 13:13; 1 Corinthians 7:17; Galatians 5:16; Ephesians 5:2, 8; Colossians 2:6 *et al.*

[44] Luke 3:4 – 6; Isaiah 40:3.

[45] John 14:6

[46] Sirkis, N., The Bible Lands Museum: Guide to the Collection, p. 125.

and consecrated things, the worth and status of an unclean person differed in no way from that of a clean person."[47]

In many ways, the principles and laws of *halaka* were directed toward the religious elite. Obermann writes, "The very term 'Pharisees' (*perusim*, 'separated, separatists') would in fact appear to have been coined first to qualify those pledged to that adherence [i.e., the Oral Law] over against the apathy of the 'common people' (*amme ha'ares*)."[48]

b. *Mikveh* or The Ritual Bath

Jews practised ritual bathing as a part of their walk with the LORD. It was and is a major aspect of *halaka*. The term *mikveh*, which describes ritual bathing, means "a collection or gathering together of water." After its reference in Genesis 1: 9 of the "gathering of waters," the *mikveh* is first mentioned in the Pentateuch in Leviticus 11:36, then in Leviticus 15:16. In Maimonides' translation, Danby notes that

> in the list of the 613 positive and negative commandments [of the *Mishnah*] prefixed to the Code, this commandment appears in the following form. "109. That purification from any uncleanness be by immersion in the waters of a *mikveh* (immersion pool), as it is said, *"He shall bathe all his flesh in water and be unclean until the even"* (Lev. 15:16). It is learned from tradition

---

[47] Herbert Danby. The Code of Maimonides Book X: The Book of Uncleanness, p.viii.

[48] Herbert Danby. op. cit., p.xiii.

that this washing shall be in water into which all of a man's body can enter at once."[49]

That ordinance was imposed on a man having had an emission of semen (sometimes referred to as "flux").

More than a millennium after the destruction of Jerusalem, when Maimonides helped to recodify *halaka* in the *Mishna Torah*, the *mikveh* as an immersion pool was commonplace throughout Israel and elsewhere in the Jewish world. *Mikveh*, however, being "a collection of water," referred to the wider use of "a gathering of water," such as a stream. A stream was preferable to a pool as water to be used for ritual washing, as will be explained. That likely is why Paul and his missionary team, when visiting Philippi for the first time, knew instinctively where to find a group of worshipping Jews and/or Jewish God-fearers on the Sabbath. It was at a riverside. Luke, in that description, says, "we expected to find a place of prayer."[50]

A river was a natural and suitable place for preparation for prayer. In the very public situation at Philippi, the persons preparing for ritual immersion – if that is what they were doing – would likely have worn some variety of costume, unlike the men who at the Ophel in Jerusalem either entered the *mikveh* naked, or like the monks at Qumran, who covered themselves with a loincloth.

Aryeh Kaplan lists the six conditions which authenticate a body of water as a *mikveh*:

> 1. The *mikveh* must consist of water. No other liquid can be used.

---

[49] Herbert Danby. op cit., p. 496.

[50] Acts 16:13.

2. The *mikveh* must either be built into the ground, or be an integral part of a building attached to the ground. It cannot consist of any vessel that can be disconnected and carried away, such as a tub, vat, or barrel.

3. The water of a *mikveh* cannot be running or flowing. The only exception to this rule is a natural spring, or a river whose water is derived mainly from springs.

4. The water of a *mikveh* cannot be drawn (*sha'uvim*). That is, it cannot be brought to the *mikveh* through direct human intervention.

5. The water cannot be channelled to the *mikveh* through anything that can become unclean (*tumeh*). For this reason, it cannot flow to the *mikveh* through pipes or vessels made of metal, clay or wood.

6. The *mikveh* must contain at least 40 *se'ah* (approximately 200 American gallons).[51]

c. The Development of *Mikve'ot*

The best of all "gathering of water" was a natural stream[52] or artesian well. It provided "living water."[53] Early in the *Torah*, the creation story includes God's description of what

---

[51] Areyeh Kaplan, op. cit., p.53

[52] This writer, preparing to enter Hezekiah's Tunnel at the Spring of Gihon in Jerusalem, happened upon a naked Jew prone in the stream, allowing the water to flow over him. He was in the process of ritual bathing for purification purposes. We apologized for the interruption and he covered up! Undoubtedly, upon our departure, he began his lustrations again.

[53] Zechariah 14:8; John 4:10; Beasley-Murray, G. R., Word Bible Commentary 36, John, p. 60.

happened in naming the bodies of water. "To the 'gathering of waters (*mikveh*)' he called seas."[54]

The absence of convenient streams imposed a hardship on Jews, so the *Oral Torah* allowed a substitute. This was problematic for Jews living in cold climates or even in communities where wadis dried up for much of the year. To meet this obvious need the Jews built *mikve'ot*. The *mikveh* needed to be large enough "for complete immersion, the tradition is to build the *mikveh* with seven steps – representing the six days of creation and the Sabbath – leading down into the pool."[55] For purposes of modesty, because a person must enter the *mikveh* naked, Jews built a construction over it, both in Herodian times and in the present time. The *mikveh* itself is based in a *bor* – "something dug," a pit.[56] Interestingly, the *mikve'ot* found at the Ophel below the Temple Mount had mostly six steps.[57]

Ritual immersion (*tevilah*) as such was the commandment of Moses.[58] *Tevilah* enabled an unclean person to become clean, and thereby permitted the worshipper to "put a person in a state of purity for the purpose of performing *mitzvot*" (God's orders).[59] The uncleanness stems from a variety of circumstances which "all revolve around loss – loss of body fluid, loss of potential

---

[54] Genesis 1:10; Aryeh Kaplan. op. cit., p. 65.

[55] Wayne Dosick, op. cit., p. 270.

[56] Ibid.

[57] Meir Ben-Dov. op. cit., p. 152.

[58] Leviticus 14:8; 15:5; 15:9; 22:6; Deuteronomy 23:12.

[59] Rabbi Wayne Dosick. op. cit., p.269

life, loss of life itself. In a state of loss, a person was not considered whole, and thus was not able to participate in ritual observances (in those days, the bringing of sacrifices to the sanctuary) with a full and complete heart."[60] Kaplan notes that it is "customary to immerse three times when going to a *mikveh*. One reason for this is because the word *mikveh* occurs three times in the *Torah*."[61]

Tevilah, therefore, was a necessary preparation for a religious or sacred duty. Early in Israelite sacrificial development, the Bible records that the high priest required purification by immersion. "Bring Aaron and his sons to the Tent of Meeting and wash them with water."[62]

This ceremony involved an agent of immersion, namely Moses. However, the purpose of this specific ritual was that of consecrating the priest and makes the involvement of an agent plausible. In subsequent passages related to *Yom Kippur*, the Day of Atonement, the high priest was to bathe (immerse) himself – no agent indicated.[63] In fact, the high priest (*Kohen Gadol*) immersed himself twice, each time after changing his sacred vestment.[64] As Dosick indicates, "here . . . the cleanliness is not physical, but an act of symbolic purification – moving from a secular role to the

---

[60] Ibid.

[61] Aryeh Kaplan. op. cit., p. 27.

[62] Exodus 29:4; 40:12; Leviticus 8:6.

[63] Leviticus 16:4, 24.

[64] Leviticus 16:5, 24.

position of priest, and moving from the ordinary tasks of the year to the holy tasks of the Yom Kippur rituals."[65]

The wilderness experience of the Israelites brought many new institutions into a bonding which allowed the descendants of Abraham to consider themselves unique. They were not only expected to immerse themselves ritually prior to the giving of the Decalogue to them; they were expected to immerse their clothing. "After Moses had gone down the mountain to the people, he consecrated them, and they washed their clothes."[66] Writes Aryeh Kaplan:

> The command to 'wash their garments' seems puzzling, until we look into the general laws regarding purification. There we find that whenever a person is required to "wash his clothing," he is also required to immerse himself in the *mikveh*. When the *Torah* states that an individual must wash his clothing, this means he must purify his clothing as well as his body in the *mikveh*. Thus, we know from tradition that an important part of the preparation for the receiving of the Ten Commandments consisted of immersion in the *mikveh*."[67]

d. The Principle of *Mikveh* Cleansing

Areyeh Kaplan points out that the commandments of the Pentateuch fall into three main categories. These are *first*, the moral and ethical laws, "the need for which," he says, "is fairly obvious."[68]

---

[65] Rabbi Wayne Dosick. op. cit. p. 269

[66] Exodus 19; 10, 14.

[67] Aryeh Kaplan, op. cit., p. 21.

[68] Aryeh Kaplan. op. cit., p. 58.

These laws deal with killing, stealing, hurting others in some way. These laws are known as the *mishpatim*, or judgments because anyone with good judgment will understand and obey them. The *second* group of commandments is known as *edos*, "witnesses." Those who follow these laws bear a witness to the faith they endorse. They are reminders of important principles, such as keeping Sabbath and Passover and other touchstones in Jewish history. The *third* group of commandments is the *chukim*, the decrees of God, whether uttered in the *Torah* or in the *Talmud*. The commandments involved in the *mikveh* are among the *chukim*.[69]

Kaplan points out that the *chukim* are the most difficult commands to keep because often their purpose is not understood. Yet the "fact that a commandment does not have an obvious reason makes its observance all the more an act of faith. It indicates we are ready and willing to obey God's commandments, even when we cannot justify them with logic. It shows that we are placing God above our own intellect."[70]

Areyeh Kaplan further explains that,

> In this spirit the Jewish people accepted the commandments. The *Torah* relates that when Israel accepted the *Torah*, their initial response was (Exodus 24:7) "All that God says we will do and we will hear (*Na'aseh VeNishma*)." Our sages stress the fact that their first statement was "we will do," and only then did they say, "we will hear." This indicates that when the *Torah* was given, we were ready to keep the commandments

---

[69] ibid.

[70] Aryeh Kaplan. op. cit., p. 8.

and "do" them, before we "heard" any reason or logic for them.

Rabbi Wayne Dosick notes that the *Torah* does not give a rationale for many of its commandments.

> While the *Torah* gives the basic rules for *kashrut* (*kosher* food laws) it does not explain *why* some animals, fish and fowl are permitted to be eaten and why others are not. It simply permits halibut but prohibits lobster; permits beef steak but prohibits bacon . . . A person learns this process: Even though those pork chops look and smell delicious, I do not eat them *because God said so.* Even though I am famished, I do not eat that ham sandwich *because God said so.* By observing the ritual laws of *kashrut* – not for any particular or logical reason, but because this is God's law for me – I am trained in the human skill of self-discipline.[71]

Sometimes the Bible gives both a command and a reason for it. As Joshua prepared to lead the children of Israel across the Jordan River into the "Promised Land," he ordered the people to take steps to prepare themselves spiritually in the quest ahead of them. Joshua instructed them: "sanctify yourselves; for tomorrow the LORD will do wonders among you."[72] That meant the people should start the ceremonial actions[73] which were necessary to present themselves as righteous before the LORD. It surely included ritual bathing. Sometimes, the bathing is only partial, *i.e.,*

---

[71] Rabbi Wayne Dosick. Living Judaism. p. 268.

[72] Joshua 3:5

[73] John Bright. The Interpreter's Bible, Vol. 2, p. 565.

hands or feet. "Sanctify yourself," (Leviticus 11:44) in this case, means washing hands before a meal.[74]

It is logical to connect the concept of sanctification with ritual bathing elsewhere in the Scriptures, even though bathing, *per se*, is not mentioned in the text. One such instance involved Samuel's visit to Jesse. The former had come to Jesse's abode to choose a king who would later replace Saul. The prophet commanded Jesse to prepare a sacrifice. "Consecrate yourselves and come to the sacrifice with me."[75] The event involved a sacrifice for which a purification rite would have been expected. The culture anticipated that to deal with holy things, such as sacrifices to the LORD, those preparing for such worship would undertake the necessary procedures to ensure their personal purification. After the consecration, then the sacrifice, Samuel proceeded to anoint David.

The *chukim* may indeed require "doing" without "hearing" (or knowing why). Nevertheless, Jewish scholars are quite ready to provide a rationale for the *mikveh* habit.

The following rationales for ritual immersion are suggested in random order. Self-immersion is, for one, an act of faith. As Dosick and Kaplan each have intimated, the individual immersing himself does so on the basis that he understands little of how the cleansing works, only that it provides an imparted righteousness to him if he properly follows the precepts. This is the Abram principle: "Go forth from your native land and from your father's house to the land that I will show you."[76] This is a walk (*halaka*) of faith.

---

[74] Abraham Cohen. Everyman's Talmud, p. 241.

[75] 1 Samuel 16:5

[76] Genesis 12:1 The Torah, A New Translation. p.20.

Secondly, ritual cleansing by immersion is an act of submission. Again, hear Aryeh Kaplan.

> When we keep commandments that have no apparent reason, we demonstrate our inner security as Jews. Even though we may not be able to justify these commandments to the world we feel secure as Jews to continue observing them. We understand what the *Torah* means when it says (Deuteronomy 4:6), "Observe and keep [the commandments], for this is your wisdom and understanding in the eyes of the nations." We do not observe the commandments because logic demands it, but simply because they were given by God. The required basis is the relationship between the commandments and their Giver. This is higher than any human wisdom.[77]

Thirdly, the *mikveh* represents an act of the creature respecting the Creator. The creature needs constant reminding of the difference between him/herself and the Creator. "The *Torah* is the means by which the Jew elevates himself back to the state of Eden," argues Kaplan. "Therefore, the Jews had to immerse in a *mikveh* before receiving the *Torah*. Through the waters of the *mikveh*, the link with Eden was reestablished."[78]

Fourthly, Jewish ritual immersion is an act of rebirth from the womb. As we will see, the concept of rebirth was basic to proselyte immersion.

> Both male and female converts immerse in a *mikveh*, a ritual pool of collected waters, as a symbolic act of ritual purification. In the waters of the *mikveh*, a proselyte is

---

[77] Aryeh Kaplan. op. cit., p. 9.

[78] Aryeh Kaplan. op. cit., p. 39.

spiritually 'reborn.' The proper blessings are recited, making the immersion a ritual act of conversion."[79]

The underlying principle of rebirth applies not only to the convert but to all who use the *mikveh*. The "sacred" water of the *mikveh* is party to a change in status in the person being immersed. The status change is from unclean (*tumeh*) to clean (*tahor*).[80] Emerging from the *mikveh* is very much like the process of a rebirth.[81]

> The *mikveh* represents the womb. When an individual enters the *mikveh*, he is re-entering the womb, and when he emerges, he is as if born anew. He attains a completely new status . . . The womb is a place that is completely divorced from all concepts of *tumah* and uncleanness. A baby enters the world in complete purity, and there is no way he can be defiled while in the womb. Thus when an individual enters the *mikveh*, he leaves all uncleanness and *tumah* behind and emerges as a new, purified person.

Aryehh Kaplan cites various authorities from the *Talmud* for his position and then writes this: "In a sense, therefore, water represents the womb of creation. When a person immerses in the *mikveh*, he is placing himself in the state of the world yet unborn, subjecting himself totally to God's creative power."[82]

---

[79] Rabbi Wayne Dosick. op. cit. p. 69.

[80] Aryeh Kaplan. op. cit., p. 12.

[81] Ibid.

[82] Aryeh Kaplan. op. cit., p. 13.

Fifthly, the *mikveh* ritual symbolizes an act of death and burial. The act of submersion becomes an act of dying and resurrection. The Hebrew word *kever* denotes both womb and grave, essentially a state of nonliving – a representation of the state of someone in the *mikveh*.[83]

> When a person immerses himself in a *mikveh*, he momentarily enters the realm of the unliving, so that when he emerges, he is like one reborn . . . To some degree, this explains why a *mikveh* . . . must be built directly in the ground, for in a sense the *mikveh* also represents the grave. When a person immerses, he is temporarily in a state of nonliving, and when he emerges, he is resurrected with a new status.[84]

Sixthly, ritual cleansing suggests that the person emerging from the *mikveh* is a new creation. Talmudic sources suggest that one immersing himself in a *mikveh* is similar to seed planting. The seeds may be ritually unclean but the plants springing from them are clean (*tahor*). The seeds had been cleansed by the ground which was their original source. The seeds which were *tumeh* died and new life which was *tahor* sprouted from them. "The same is true of man. For him, the waters of the *mikveh* are his womb and source, and when he emerges, he too is like a new individual."[85]

When a person immerses himself, either before, after or during the ritual (depending on regional tradition), he/she will say, "Blessed are You, O Lord, our God, King of the

---

[83] Aryeh Kaplan. op. cit. p. 14.

[84] Ibid.

[85] Ibid.

universe, who has sanctified us with your commandments and commanded us concerning immersion."

3. Proselyte Initiation and Ritual Bathing

An alien (*ger*) who wanted to become a Jew was also obliged to participate in a "conversion immersion." That the Jewish law allowed such a conversion is astonishing in itself. The *Torah* commanded that the children of Israel give basic human rights to aliens who kept company with them and were spiritually sensitive to monotheistic beliefs. This was a reminder of how hospitality given by aliens should be honoured and reciprocated.[86]

Aliens were permitted to celebrate the great festivals of Israel – if they conformed to the Israelite rules. The rules included circumcision of all males in the alien's household.[87] Circumcision was likewise obligatory for persons (and their male children) desirous of "becoming Jews" . . . No one could celebrate the Passover without having been circumcised. Ritual circumcision for Gentiles already circumcised was and is known as *dam bris*, "the blood of the covenant."[88]

Tevilah was likewise obligatory. A Jew born from the seed of Israel had an option of being observant or unobservant. He was born a Jew and could not lightly be disconnected from his ancestry. On the other hand, someone who asked to become a Jew had no choice but to be observant. So, to become a new person, he submitted himself not only to the circumcision covenant ritual but also to the

---

[86] Exodus 18:3; Deuteronomy 14:21; Numbers 9:14.

[87] Numbers 9:14; Exodus 12:43-49.

[88] Aryeh Kaplan. op. cit., p. 21.

symbols attached to the *mikveh*. A male convert is called a *ger*; a female convert is called a *giyoret*.[89] The Bible tells of Ruth, a Moabitess, who converted to the faith of her mother-in-law. Rabbi Dosick describes Ruth as "the prototype proselyte – adopting the Jewish God and the Jewish People as her own with sincerity, determination and joy."[90]

Proselyte ritual washing was more complicated than that of someone born a Jew. First, the would-be convert had to urge the rabbi to accept him.[91] Prior to the Christian era, Jews accepted proselytes with greater ease. Scriptural injunctions prepared the way for aliens to become Jews. Despite some prohibitions, some aliens intermarried with the Israelites. "Intermarrieds ought to be seen as potential converts," writes Michael Lerner about couples who have one partner from outside Judaism. "Rather than be treated as betrayers, the intermarried couple that starts to attend synagogue or other Jewish religious observances ought to be enthusiastically welcomed."[92]

Rabbis were not uniformly in agreement about procedures required of proselytes. Individual schools among the Pharisees offered differing advice on how to process proselytes into the faith. Consider the comments proposed by Joachim Jeremias.

It was in Jerusalem during the last three decades BC that there were three Gentiles converted to Judaism, who

---

[89] Rabbi Wayne Dosick. op cit. p., 65.

[90] Ibid.

[91] Ibid.

[92] Michael Lerner. op. cit., p. 277.

were rejected by Shammai but welcomed by Hillel. Another event, recorded in connection with a dispute between the schools of Shammai and Hillel, belongs to the period of AD 30. The Shammaites declared admissible the baptism of a convert on the day of his circumcision, but the Hillelites required an interval of seven days between circumcision and baptism . . . because they attributed to the Gentile the same impurity as a corpse.[93]

Within the *Torah*, the stage was set for outsiders (those who had no one to speak for them by virtue of their status) to become Jews. "He defends the cause of the fatherless and the widow and the alien, giving him food and clothing. And you are to love those who are aliens for you yourselves were aliens in Egypt."[94] Isaiah prophesied,

Foreigners who bind themselves to the LORD to serve him, to love the name of the LORD, and to worship him, all who keep the Sabbath without desecrating it and who hold fast to my covenant – these will I bring to my holy mountain and give them joy in my house of prayer. Their burnt offerings and sacrifices will be accepted on my altar; for my house will be called a house of prayer for all nations.[95]

A convert to Judaism first submitted himself for test questions. He must face a three-man tribunal (*beit den*) to adjudicate his worthiness to advance as a proselyte. Aryeh Kaplan comments, "Unless done in the presence of such a

---

[93] Joachim Jeremias. Jerusalem in the Time of Jesus, p. 321.

[94] Deuteronomy 10:18, 19.

[95] Isaiah 56:6, 7.

court, the conversion is not valid."[96] If he answered the authority appropriately, he could move on to the next stages of conversion, the understanding of covenant obligations, followed by purification rituals. The *beit den* would then examine him for basic Jewish knowledge, commitment to the commandments of the *Torah* and *Oral Torah* and identity with the rituals and peoplehood of Judaism.[97] At the ceremony's conclusion, the *beit den* would sign a document approving that the candidate had become a Jew.

An examining council asks each proselyte candidate for his commitment to Jewish requirements. Does he realize how Jews have been treated and suffered for their faith? He is reminded that in his past, he (she) partook of forbidden food, profaned Sabbath rules, and in short, acted like a Gentile. After promising to keep the kosher and Sabbath rules (and other ways which define a Jew's *halaka*) the candidate is warned of dire penalties which will befall a proselyte if he repeats such as he did in his pre-Jewish living. In the same way he is informed of the punishments attached to the precepts, he is likewise informed of the benefits. He is told that in the next world he will be among the righteous. The examining council will not overstate the negatives. If the candidate accepts, he is circumcised immediately. After he is healed, he undergoes immersion in a *mikveh* without delay. Two disciples of the rabbinical stand along him, instructing "him in the minor and more important precepts. When he has immersed himself and ascended from the water he is an Israelite in every respect" (Jeb. 47b).[98]

---

[96] Aryeh Kaplan. op. cit., p. 22.

[97] Rabbi Wayne Dosick. op. cit., p.69.

[98] Abraham Cohen. op cit. p. 64, 65.

The candidate then immerses himself in the *mikveh*. It is his/her witness to being "reborn."[99] The convert takes on a Jewish identity as a son or daughter of Abraham and takes on a Jewish name. The language of death, womb, birth, resurrection and change of status are especially pertinent in this situation. "Our sages teach us," writes Aryeh Kaplan, that the word *mikveh* has the same letters as *ko(v)mah*, the Hebrew words for 'rising,' or 'standing tall.' It is through the *mikveh* that man can rise from things associated with his fallen state, and re-establish a link with the perfected state that is Eden.[100]

Michael Lerner writes of modern conversions,

> After the convert completes the *mikveh* immersion and dresses s/he goes to a place in which the community forms a circle into which s/he is welcomed. Each person in the circle addresses the convert by her/his new Jewish name offers words of welcome and then the community says a prayer and joins in song and celebration of the happy event.[101]

In biblical times more was yet required of proselytes. For that matter, more was required of "natural" Jews who were required to ensure that their eating utensils were also properly purified. The challenge to them came from the *Torah* when Eleazar, the priest, ordered the soldiers fighting

---

[99] Rabbi Wayne Dosick. op. cit. p. 69.

[100] Aryeh Kaplan. op. cit., p. 36.

[101] Michael Lerner. Jewish Renewal, p. 277.

44

the Mideanites to purify their garments and their cooking vessels with water.[102]

This commandment became the norm for dish purification by converts. Everything in life, is sacred to a Jew and thus everything he uses should be sanctified. The rabbinic spin on this does not follow from a biblical explanation. Rabbi Samson Raphael Hirsch explains

> that a metal utensil is therefore the most visible sign of man's intelligent mastery over the earth and its materials. Not only the shape but the use of the material itself proclaims this fact . . . *tumah*. The *Torah* requires, however, that even the most physical of man's activities be elevated to the realm of the spiritual. Before using a metal utensil for eating, we must first sanctify and elevate it to a level of holiness by immersion in a *mikveh*. The vessel will, in turn, sanctify the food served in it. In this manner, a Jew's eating utensils become like consecrated vessels in the Holy Temple, which sanctified anything that was placed in them.[103]

If a Jew needed to immerse his created vessels in a *mikveh*, how much more important it was for a convert to purify his dishes. They had been previously used to prepare and serve unclean food. Thus, the dishes required ritual immersion as well.

Evidently, proselytes' offspring also were immersed at the time of the parents' conversion. However, children born

---

[102] Numbers 31:21–24.

[103] Aryeh Kaplan. op. cit., p. 26.

after their parents' conversion were treated normally as Jews and were not immersed as converts.[104]

4. Women and Ritual Cleansing

In the long list of reasons for necessary immersion, women's requirements were especially important. *Tevilah* was important for women because of menstruation and birthing. In Herodian times when the Temple was intact, women had a different access to the Temple than did the men. Priests also used a separate *mikveh*.[105] Men entered the Temple complex from below, via the *mikve'ot*, through the three doors of the Hulda (Chulda) Gates passing through the 100 metre-long Hulda tunnel and stairs which brought them to the Temple grounds.

Upon leaving the Temple Mount, the men made an exit through double doors a few metres west of the Hulda Gates. The exit was called "the Double Gate," or "the Hulda Exit."[106]

Women, however, were prohibited from using the same entrance as the men. Women were not allowed to mingle with men during sacred proceedings.[107] Indeed, women were given a separate part of the temple for their own sacrificial purposes. It is not clear that they were allowed to make

---

[104] Dale Moody. Review and Expositor: Baptists and Baptism, Vol. LXV. No. 1., p. 2.

[105] Rabbi Leibel Reznick. The Holy Temple Revisited, p. 103.

[106] Rabbi Leibel Reznick. op. cit., pp. 44,45.

[107] Rabbi Leibel Reznick. op. cit., p. 84.

sacrifices but at least, like non-priest males, they could participate by watching.[108]

Admission to the Temple precincts was a very special reason for anyone to undergo ritual immersion. The Temple area was not the only place for *tevilah*. Indeed, observant Jews everywhere practise immersion routinely as a part of their devotion to God. Thus the *mikve'ot* in communities around Herodian Israel and now throughout the world! Ritual immersion was a stern requirement for observant female Jews.

A Jewish girl became a woman at age twelve plus one day.[109] A boy became a man a year later. (At 13 years of age, a male was considered of age to fulfil the commandments – a *bar mitzah*.)[110] A female, however, despite the 12 year and a day general rule, was judged to be truly of age by her menstrual activity. If she was under 12 and she had three "periods," that sufficed to require her to immerse ritually in the *mikveh*.[111]

If she was *niddah*, the Jewish term used to describe a woman in estrus, she was required to touch no man, including her husband. If her period lasted seven days – and she had to ensure that the menstruation indeed had stopped – she needed seven more days free of vaginal bleeding before she could ritually cleanse herself by *tevilah*.[112] The test of

---

[108] Rabbi Leibel Reznick. op. cit., p. 83.

[109] Rabbi Binyomin Forst. The Laws of Niddah, p. 181.

[110] Abraham Cohen. op. cit., p. 73.

[111] Rabbi Binyomin Forst. op. cit., p. 181 (see note 19).

[112] Leviticus 15:19; 25–28; 18:5 – 9.

stopped bleeding was on a pad or cloth *(hefseik taharah)*. Isaiah referred to the menstrual cloths as "filthy rags."[113] The filthiness had less to do with the hygiene and much more to do with the ritual status of *niddah*.

During the time the woman was *niddah*, she could have not contact of any kind with her husband or any man. She was to keep her state of *niddah* her secret, known only to her husband. She could not communicate her state with any other person and could immerse herself for purification only when she was assured that no one knew of her visit to the *mikveh*. At that, among those who might know, they were required to keep their own counsel on this knowledge.[114]

Many are the regulations imposed upon women for ritual purity. They need not be listed in this document but they were considered necessary in biblical times as well as in the current traditions of Judaism (among observant Jews). Measurements for immersion are as exactly as they are for men.

A woman is required to immerse at least twice to ensure that the natural folds in her body are completely washed in the *mikve'ot*'s water – usually after nightfall. She must be naked. As a prelude to ritual immersion, she should take a regular bath to clean herself hygienically and distinguish body care from spiritual care. In the *mikveh*, she must ensure that her hair is totally immersed and so may take an observer with her to the *mikveh* to make sure she is totally submerged. She must not look unduly at her genital region and should roil the waters as to make such personal

---

[113] Isaiah 64:6.

[114] Harav Mordechai Eliyahu. The Laws of Niddah and Family Purity, p. 166.

inspection more difficult. If she cannot completely submerge herself in a stream (as over against a ground *mikveh*), she is permitted to lie prone so that the water runs completely over her.[115]

Ideally, the married woman is ritually pure before *Shabbat*. Her husband likewise would have purified himself in a *mikveh*. To obey the *mitzvah* (God's commandment) of procreation, the two would have intercourse that night – preferably after midnight. The next morning the man needed to immerse himself in a *mikveh*.[116]

The laws of *niddah* prohibiting contact with a man, also provided a form of birth control. Counting the 14 days from her original menstruation, the woman was ideally fertile by the time she resumed normal marital relations. That meant her chances of conceiving a child were unusually high for she was at her most fertile stage of her cycle. The laws of *niddah*, effectively ensured procreation within the Jewish ethnic group.

One may, therefore, read the story of David and Bathsheba in a different light. When David, from his palace balcony, espied Bathsheba bathing, it was evening, the prime time to use her *mikveh*. She was naked, as she would have been to use a *mikveh*. The Scripture told that "she had purified herself from her uncleanness."[117] She was exceptionally vulnerable to conceive – which she did when David summoned her to his palace and had intercourse with her. Thus, David not only committed adultery with her, not only arranged for the murder of her husband, not only broke

---

[115] Harav Moshe David Tendler. op. cit., pp. 28 – 34.

[116] Harav Mordechai Eliyahu. op. cit., pp. 203, 204.

[117] 2 Samuel 11:4c.

the commandment to not covet his neighbour's wife, but he profaned her most personal aspects of *halaka*, her spiritual "walk with God."

The laws of *niddah* concerning vaginal discharge required a woman to accept her "uncleanness" until the discharge stopped.[118] After seven "clear" days she could proceed to the *mikveh* for the purification process.

In the biblical story of a haemorrhaging woman approaching Jesus, the principle of *niddah* is at work. She touched Jesus' garment which would have made him "unclean" but Jesus disregarded that factor and turned his attention to helping the desperate woman.[119] She then would have been able to visit a *mikveh* seven days later and participate in normative life without the stigma of being unclean or impure.[120] Therefore her healing was doubled. She was healed of the bleeding disorder and she was cured of her social stigma. The Bible leaves unsaid what Jesus did about "ritually purifying" himself after she had touched him but undoubtedly the scandal mongers took note of it.

Did the disciples ritually purify themselves? The Bible also may connect the events of the Upper Room and Last Supper with a baptismal or immersion ritual. The Fourth Gospel recounts that Jesus took a bowl and began to wash the disciples' feet as an acted parable of servanthood.[121] Peter protested that he would not allow someone superior to do that for him – he hinted it was a slave's work to wash

---

[118] Leviticus 15:25–28.

[119] Mark 5:25 ff.

[120] Harav Moshe David Tendler. Pardes Rimonim. p. 16

[121] John 13:1–20.

feet. Jesus corrected Peter's protest. A disciple's work like Messiah's, Jesus proposed, is servant work. Jesus said to Peter, "Unless I wash you, you have no part of me!"[122]

Jesus' comments raise not a few questions. In addition to telling Peter that discipleship meant a bondservant ministry, was Jesus projecting that baptism "in his name"[123] was essential also for discipleship? Or was this a comment that the ritual immersions with which Peter surely was familiar and used to, were like the old wineskins and old cloth[124] of an outworn religious tradition?

The Upper Room meal may or may not have been a *seder*.[125] Numerous suggestions on this prove nothing about the actual date of the Lord's Supper.[126] Another dating suggests that this supper took place on the eve, i.e., the day before the Passover. The dating is less important than the idea of ritually preparing for Passover in Jerusalem by using the *mikveh*.

The *mikve'ot* of the Ophel would have been unusually busy with the hordes of Diaspora pilgrims coming to attend the feast, plus the many observant Jews living in and around Jerusalem. Presumably the disciples, together with Jesus, would have frequented the Ophel's ritual baths on that day,

---

[122] John 13:8.

[123] Acts 2:38.

[124] Matthew 9:16; 17.

[125] Luke 22:7; Matthew 26:18–19.

[126] G. R Beasley-Murray. Word Bible Commentary (Second Edition)Volume 36: John. Nashville: Thomas Nelson Publishers, 1999. p. 224, 225.

certainly if it was Passover or whether the eve of Passover. After all, the "Jesus group" likely had been to the Temple earlier in the day as they travelled from Bethany into Jerusalem.

Jesus commented on Peter's refusal to let Jesus wash his feet. "A person who has had a bath needs only to wash his feet; his whole body is clean. And you are clean, though not every one of you."

Matthew's record suggests Jesus used two different Greek (it begs the question of whether Jesus spoke Aramaic or Greek) words for "wash." In referring to the "bath," he used the verb *louō*. In referring to the hands and feet, Jesus used the verb *niptō*. Employed in the Bible, *louō* refers somewhat to purifying ablutions, as in Ephesians 3:26 where the noun form is translated as cleansing. It meant washing the entire body. The verb *niptō*, on the other hand, refers to washing parts of the body, as in Matthew 6:17.

This passage implies very strongly that Peter recently had immersed himself in a *mikveh* and was ritually clean. In this verbal interchange with Peter, Jesus was not commenting of the efficacy of the ritual bath. Rather, Jesus noted that Peter's response was an overreaction to Jesus' ministry of servanthood in the foot washing of the Upper Room.

This passage and many others, such as Nicodemus' night meeting with Jesus, can be interpreted more richly in light of the Jewish *tevilah*. The Nicodemus' encounter will be discussed more fully in chapter 5. Many biblical passages indicate that the forms, mode and sometimes even the words associated with the *mikveh* ritual bear strong similarities to what later became Christian baptism.

CHAPTER 2

Ritual Washings at Qumran and Masada

One other aspect of *tevilah* requires consideration. Ritual washings took place at Qumran near Jericho and overlooking the northern end of the Dead Sea. Qumran had been inhabited since the sixth century BC. It became a monastic community during the Maccabean period and survived on rainwater for its only source of water.[127] Specific to the activity of the Qumranites was its unique form of *tevilah*.

This is the special act of ritual washings which became a part of the daily habits of the Qumranites. The residents of Qumran held two significant rituals which were similar, yet dissimilar to the Christian undertakings of baptism and communion. The Qumran refectory was a special place of sacrament, where the leader/priest of the sect said prayers over the communal meal and anticipated the end times to whose symbol the meal pointed.[128]

---

[127] Kathleen M. Kenyon,. The Bible & Recent Archaeology, p. 93.

[128] G Vermes. The Dead Sea Scrolls in English, p. 81.

Generally, the Qumranites were loosely identified as a branch of the Essene movement.[129] The Essenes were no monolithic community. Evidently they lived at the edge of many Jewish villages and in Jerusalem may have had "a quarter" and an entrance to the city known as the Essene Gate on Mount Zion (now within the property of the American School). Speculation suggests that some of the inhabitants of the Essene Quarter were outcasts from Qumran during the reign of Herod the Great.[130]

Whether this expulsion derived from a schism within Qumran, as Murphy-O'Connor intimates,[131] or due to the earthquake of 31 BC,[132] which for 30 years emptied Qumran of its monks, is a matter of question. Some *mikve'ot* have been unearthed in Jerusalem's Essene Quarter in the mid-1980s. One was uncovered at the beginning of the 20th century.[133]

---

[129] Norman Golb. Who Wrote the Dead Sea Scrolls? New York: Scribner. 1995. pp. 100 – 115; Schiffman, Lawrence H. Reclaiming the Dead Sea Scrolls. New York: Doubleday, 1995. p .79.

[130] Jerome Murphy-O'Connor. Oxford Archaeological Guides: The Holy Land. Oxford: Oxford University Press, 1998. p. 107.

[131] Ibid.

[132] J. T. Milik,. Ten Years of Discovery in the Wilderness of Judaea. London: SCM Press Ltd., 1959. p. 52.

[133] James H. Charlesworth. (ed.). Jesus and the Dead Sea Scrolls. New York: Doubleday, 1992. p. 213.

In the Qumran Community, residents fitted into four categories of participants, depending upon how recently or how long they had been in the fellowship. The leadership represented the hierarchy of the priesthood which dominated life at Qumran, even though no sacrifices, as such, likely took place there. The purifications preceding the substitute sacrificial meal were adhered to carefully. Frequent washings were the norm. The communal meal seems to have been the substitute for a Temple sacrifice. Washings were required as a purity prerequisite to eating.[134]

1. Discovery of the Scrolls

The Essenes and the Qumran community may have been a historical footnote except for the discovery, in 1947, of long-hidden scrolls. Previously, these ascetics were known to scholars primarily through the writings of Philo and Josephus. They were known for seeking purity and their exclusiveness.

Some Essenes possibly domiciled near Damascus,[135] others in Jerusalem, in small villages of Palestine and at Qumran. They hid the scrolls in caves near Qumran, an archaeological ruin at the northwest edge of the Dead Sea

---

[134] Marcel Simon. Jewish Sects at the Time of Jesus, p. 75.

[135] Lawrence H. Schiffman. Reclaiming the Dead Sea Scrolls. New York: Doubleday. 1995, p. 94. Schiffman suggests that Damascus is likely a "code word" for Qumran, thus the *Damascus Document*.

some 1,000 feet above it. The site is on a plateau at the eastern limit of the Wilderness of Judea.[136]

The way in which the scrolls were found is relatively well-known. In brief, a young shepherd named Mohammad ed-Di'b began whiling away his time by tossing stones near the cliff opposite Qumran, one stone of which went into a hole or cave and created a breaking sound. At first startled, then curious, he returned a day later with his cousin Ahmad Mohammad. Together they climbed to the cave to see what had happened. They found some broken jars and some others which were intact. Inside the unbroken jars they found scrolls, brought them to their uncle, who some weeks later sold them to an antiquities dealer in Bethlehem – Halil Iskandar Sahin.[137]

The story, however, has more intrigue to it than that. Some Bedouins clandestinely began to search the caves and found more fragments of manuscripts, offering them for sale at reasonable prices to scholars and scholastic institutions in Jerusalem.

Eventually, E. L. Sukenik, a professor at Jerusalem's Hebrew University[138] (and father of Yigael Yadin) bought three manuscripts and spirited them from Bethlehem to Jerusalem under a cloak of secrecy. Clandestine efforts were necessary because of the Arab-Jewish struggles in 1947 and 1948. Jurisdictions changed because of politics and belligerence between the ethnic groups in their struggle for nationhood. Israel declared itself to be a nation. Jordan likewise came into existence. In 1948 a truce allowed

---

[136] J. T. Milik. op. cit. p. 11.

[137] J. T. Milik. op. cit. pp.11–13.

[138] Ibid.

archaeologists to investigate Qumran and the desert cave areas under the protection of the newly-formed Jordanian Department of Antiquities. After the "Six Day War" of 1967 the area was seized by Israel.

In 1949 the cave was found again, and its clearing began under the aegis of the Jordanian Department of Antiquities, the École Biblique et Archéologique Française de Jérusalem, and the Palestine Archaeological Museum with some assistance from the American School of Oriental Research in Jerusalem. Father Roland de Vaux of the École Biblique and G. Lankester Harding at the Jordanian Department of Antiquities supervised the excavations.[139]

As time progressed, many more caves in the general area of Qumran were found, some due to tips from "old-timers," to contain more caches of valuable manuscripts. Among them were the treasured fragments and scrolls of Caves IV and V[140] and their discovery called for a larger team of experts to preserve and interpret them. Collectively, the discoveries became known as the Dead Sea Scrolls.

Father Jean Danielou was visiting Qumran in 1952. He had been told that no further discoveries would be expected. But it didn't happen that way. He recalled:

I was at Qumran on September 1 of that same year, and Father de Vaux told me it looked as though there would be no further finds. A fortnight later the Bedouins discovered Cave 4, the richest of all. Finally, seven other

---

[139] Ibid.

[140] John Allegro. The Dead Sea Scrolls. London: Penguin Books. 1956, 1964, 1990. p. 45.

caves containing fragments of lesser importance were also discovered.[141]

The scrolls were extraordinarily valuable on many fronts. For example, they provided a great number of manuscripts which were dated prior to the Masoretic texts.[142] They produced a complete scroll of Isaiah in Hebrew dated from the first century AD. They provided commentaries on biblical books, such as Habakkuk.

In later finds from caves along the cliffs southward from Qumran, dated in the second century AD, the Qumranites issued marriage, social and business contracts. From them the scholars learned greater insight into how life was conducted in the social order of the day. But for purposes of this writing, the caves produced material which illuminated the beliefs and actions of the Dead Sea Sect regarding ritual washings. David Flusser declares this sect, without doubt, to be Essenes.[143]

Thus the caves provided a detailed and defined insight into the Essene movement, especially at Qumran. The scrolls likewise replaced the insights of Josephus and Philo as the chief reporters of Essene ways. They further illuminated the knowledge of religious and social life in Israel during Herodian and early Christian times.

---

[141] Jean Danielou. The Dead Sea Scrolls and Primitive Christianity. New York: New American Library (Helicon Press 1958), 1962. p. 13.

[142] Lawrence H. Schiffman. op. cit. New York: Doubleday, 1995. pp. 170–180.

[143] David Flusser. The Spiritual History of the Dead Sea Sect. Tel Aviv: Mod Books. 1989. p. 33.

The caves' several scrolls' reference to immersion and repentance advanced a possibility that John the Baptist was somehow connected to the Qumran sect and possibly Jesus himself. The scrolls begged the comparison of Jesus' teachings and those of the Essenes as well as John's baptismal practices. As studies advanced, parallels of the Christian Eucharist and the monks' communal meal began to be examined.

In the theology of the Qumranites the meal anticipated a banquet to which the "elect" would be invited. Marcel Simon proposed what could be a disputed understanding, that the banquet presider would be the "Messiah of Aaron, of the tribe of Levi, the eschatological High Priest, spiritual leader of the community."[144]

As Marcel Simon has observed:

"It is the priest who shall bless the first fruits of bread and wine, and shall stretch out his hand over the bread. And afterwards, all the Congregation of the Community shall bless, each according to this rite at every meal where at least ten persons are assembled" (Society Manuel Annex 2:19-22). Apparently this is simply the customary Essenian ritual, transposed into an eschatological framework. Consequently, we are justified in assuming that the daily cultic meal of Qumran is an anticipation of the messianic banquet, in the same way that the whole organization of the Essene sect is a prefiguration of the coming kingdom.[145]

---

[144] Marcel Simon. op. cit., p. 78.

[145] Ibid.

2. Ritual Purity at Qumran

The Qumran Community was not an example of traditional Judaism. It was something of an aberration. Max I. Dimont describes their place in Judaism this way: "The Pharisees . . . looked upon the Sadducees as conservatives, upon the Essenes as zealots, and upon themselves as liberals."[146] The general consensus among scholars is that the Qumranites were Essenes who had separated themselves from the Jerusalem Temple cult.[147]

The sectarians at Qumran thought of themselves as the pure Israel. The Essenes originated from the opposition of some purists to the Hasmonean House which had replaced the Seleucid governors of "Palestine." The Hasmoneans united the titles of king and high priest. Alexander Jannaeus, a warrior, dared to offer sacrifices at the Temple in Jerusalem. This abomination caused a revolt among the religious leaders of Judaism.

The end result was the withdrawal from religious rites at the Temple by purists like the practitioners who later would become the Essene movement. This group considered the mixture of politics and Temple rites to be illegitimate. Therefore, they thought such illegitimacy polluted all rites and sacrifices at the Temple. Their solution was to withdraw.[148] Some of them withdrew to Qumran.

---

[146] Max I. Dimont. Jews, God and History, p. 88.

[147] Leonard F. Badia. Qumran Baptism and John the Baptist's Baptism, p. 2.

[148] John Allegro,. op. cit. pp. 106–109.

In 1981, in an interview for a documentary[149] produced for and aired on Canadian television, Yigael Yadin – archaeologist, army general, scholar, and Israeli former deputy prime minister – told this writer his opinion that the separation began in the second century BC and allowed the Essenes to develop an *ad hoc* theology to suitably bypass the need for the sacrificial system. The Dead Sea enterprise was an "interim solution." Commenting on the communal meal which appears so similar to the Communion which Christians celebrate, he stated,

> This is one of the most fascinating aspects of the possible connections between the Dead Sea Scrolls and Christianity because obviously . . . with the Essenes, the communal meal was a very holy affair. The priest had to say the grace on the bread and on the wine before everybody started. This goes back to at least the second century BC. Of course there are lots of similarities between that and the Eucharist and many scholars point that out. There is an obvious possible influence between the two. Obviously, in this case, the Essenes were the first.

Because the Qumranites were obsessed with being the pure Israel, much of their focus was on ways to ensure their purity. They would not use oil, believing it to "transmit ritual impurity from one container to another." They esteemed humility as a desirable virtue.[150] They believed that amassing goods was wrong and that assets should be shared

---

[149] Paradox: Born King., aired CTV Toronto, January 1982. [In McMaster Divinity College Baptist Archives]

[150] James M. Charlesworth. op. cit. p. 15.

with the poor and for common use.[151] Use of things was communal but ownership was private. The Sabbath was a special day to the monks and they honoured it diligently and respectfully with appropriate restrictions in activity and conversation. On the Sabbath the monks avoided making a bowel movement.[152]

To ensure such purity, the group created a system of punishments and penances for breaking the code of conduct known as the *Rule of the Community*. Fines for breaking the *Rule* varied from outright permanent expulsion from the sect to what was more common, a rationing of food. More severe fines included separation from solid food for one to two years for rebelling against the community. The least fine included reduction of food rations by one-fourth for 10 days.[153] The latter penance was imposed for "interrupting one's fellow, absence without reason from the assembly for three sessions and gesticulating with one's left hand during conversation.[154] The [left] hand was the "toilet" hand.

On this note the matter of toilet cleanliness was exceedingly important. Josephus noted that the Essenes dug a trench a foot deep with a hatchet, and modestly covered themselves as they voided or relieved themselves. They treated such bodily functions, not simply as a matter of

---

[151] Lawrence H. Schiffman. op. cit., p. 110.

[152] James C. VanderKam. The Dead Sea Scrolls Today. Grand Rapids MI: William B. Eerdmans Publishing Company, 1994. p. 86; Yancey, Philip. The Jesus I Never Knew. Grand Rapids MI: Zondervan Publishing House, 1995, p. 61.

[153] Lawrence H. Schiffman. op. cit., p. 109.

[154] Ibid.

hygiene, but as a righteous defilement. Therefore, they had to immerse themselves after toilet use for the sake of ritual purity.[155] The *War Rule* indicated that the latrine (literally: the place of the [left] hand) should be 2,000 cubits distance from the "camp."[156] James VanderKam offers a rationalization for the distance, hinting that a Sabbath day's journey was a factor. The *Temple Scroll* offers a longer walk to the latrine, 3,000 cubits, so that it was out of sight lines from the Qumranite settlement. Yet, in Jerusalem, at the Essene Quarter, the presence of walls and gate made a difference in the distances to the latrine and shortened them.

> It has often been noted that, as the Sabbath limit for a journey was two thousand cubits, the Essenes had to plan carefully so as not to defile the seventh day. Yigael Yadin has argued that the Essene Gate in Jerusalem was so situated that it would be an appropriate distance from the communal "place of the [left] hand."[157]

Water was a symbol of purity to the Qumranites, in the same way that it was in traditional Judaism. The ablutions to ensure ritual purity were therefore taken most seriously. Water was precious in such an arid area of the country, but the Essenes took elaborate pains to gather and husband the water from the rare rainfalls and the nearby Wadi.

The monks must have consumed much water just in drinking and for hygiene. By far, however, the most important water of Qumran was that which was consecrated for purification. As Lawrence Schiffman points out:

---

[155] James C. VanderKam. op. cit. p. 86.

[156] Ibid.

[157] Ibid.

Ritual purity was greatly emphasized. Ablutions were required not only before communal meals but also after relieving oneself and after coming in contact with a nonmember or a novice. Members were extremely careful about attending to natural functions modestly. They immersed often in order to maintain ritual purity and refrained from expectorating. They customarily wore white garments regarding modesty of dress as very important. Noteworthy was their stringency in Sabbath observance.[158]

A more proactive approach to personal purity was the monks availing themselves of the purifying bath. On one hand, the exclusivity of the sect disallowed novices even to use the *mikve'ot*. They were deemed unworthy of it and would contaminate the sanctity of the "holy" water.

Some disagreement about possible *mikve'ot* at Qumran centres around the possibility that the community's various pools and cisterns were not necessarily used for complete immersion ritual bathing. While several scholars agree that ritual immersions took place at Qumran, others suggest that the Qumranites conducted their baptismal and ablution rites at the Jordan River or a wadi (Ain Feshkha) nearby Qumran.[159] Maybe that was just for the immersion of novices. The difficulty with the alternative suggestion is that the Qumranites placed such a high importance on ritual, moral and ethical purity, that the necessarily very frequent ablutions required a conveniently adjacent immersion pool. The Jordan River required a five-hour hike from Qumran.

---

[158] Lawrence H. Schiffman. op. cit. p. 80.

[159] Leonard Badia. op cit., pp. 10, 11, 15.

Certainly, the Qumranites constantly frequented their *mikveh*. Initiation required a baptism, not just *tevilah*.[160] Baptism required confession and admission of sins; *tevilah* did not. Simon suggests that "perhaps the baptism of new members [to the community] consisted simply of admitting them for the first time to the normal immersions of the sect."[161]

Father Jean Danielou harbours similar thoughts on the importance of initiation into the community through the initial immersion. The rite of initiation may simply have been an admission procedure to the purification rituals practised by the monks.

> The Essian baptism was nothing more than admission to the daily baths of the community after a yearlong novitiate. There are no indications that the first immersion had any special significance.[162]

The regular bathing of the monks, however, had other dimensions to it. It was eschatologically connected. Bathing admitted the monk to the communal meal, which, as has been noted, was the monks' daily foretaste of a future end-times banquet.

Schiffman proposes:

> The idea that one should prepare himself for the end of the world by doing penance is a familiar one in the Qumran scrolls. The sons of Zadok actually call themselves The Penitents. Further, they form a

---

[160] Marcel Simon. op. cit., p. 75.

[161] Ibid.

[162] Jean Danielou. op. cit. p. 23.

community of penitents; and the act of baptism constitutes entry to the community. And this is an extremely interesting point. One cannot help but be struck by the importance that ritual ablutions have for the sectarians of Qumran and for John, called the Baptist, and his followers. It is difficult not to think that there must have been a certain connection between the two practices.[163]

The immersions of the sect were somewhat different from what was practised in more official circles of Second Temple Judaism. Certainly, the Essenes practised the same purification rites but they attached a somewhat different theological importance to them. Purification to the Qumranites was only effective if it was accompanied by moral and ethical repentance.[164]

Even here, the precise meanings of "washings" are not unanimous among Qumran scholars. Schiffman[165] points out that "ritual purity and impurity were symbolic manifestations of the moral and religious state of the individual."[166] Schiffman quotes the *Rule of the Community* 3:4–6 to underline the importance of personal repentance:

He will not be purified by atonement rituals,
nor will he become pure in waters of lustration.
He will not be sanctified in seas or rivers,
nor will he be purified in any waters of ablution.

---

[163] Jean Danielou. op. cit. p. 21.

[164] G. Vermes. op. cit. Penguin Books version), p. 79.

[165] Lawrence Schiffman, op. cit., p. 103.

[166] Lawrence H. Schiffman. op. cit., p. 103.

Impure, impure he will remain as along as he despises regulations, so as not to be disciplined by the counsel of His community.[167]

Candidates wishing to enter the Qumranite community were faced with the reality of the sect's austere life. That great high wall of personal cost prevented many hopefuls of ever getting past the symbolic gate of self-denial. They were told they were impure – only a dead body was more defiled[168] – and needed a year's preparation before even being considered for initiation by immersion in the *mikveh*. The candidate had to study Essene teachings and rules for a year. As a prospective member, he received basic Qumranite equipment, such as a loincloth, a white garment and the traditional Qumranite hatchet for digging a latrine. After a satisfactory novitiate, the candidate was allowed to enter the next phase of Essene life.

John Allegro has written about this initiation and baptism at Qumran as follows:

This rite of initiation into the full membership of the Community was probably accompanied by an initial baptism ceremony. Whether or not they used the great cisterns at the Qumran Settlement for this purpose is still open to question . . . Certainly this would accord with the injunction of the *Damascus Document* that no man shall bathe in water of less depth than that required to cover a person, but whether this ruling had relevance to baptismal ceremonies is not clear. It seems more probable in some ways that the Sect would prefer the traditional running water of the Jordan River not so far away, or nearer still the clear waters of 'Ain Feskha' –

---

[167] Ibid.

[168] Lawrence H. Schiffman. op. cit. p. 102.

although at present these would only 'cover a man' if he were lying down. We know very little about the actual baptismal ceremony, although some fragments from the Fourth Cave tell us something about the benedictions used at this rite. Once a person had been admitted to the Purity of the Many he could be baptized in the same water as other full members, but the Sect was careful that no novitiate or nonmember was allowed to touch this water, nor any of his possessions, since he was ritually "unclean"[169]. . .

"Let him (the sinner) not enter the water to come into touch with the purity of holy men. For such shall not be cleansed until they have repented of their wickedness; for uncleanness is on all transgressors of his word."[170]

After a year of waiting, "The Many" allowed the candidate to enter a further probationary phase, normally, another full year. He was permitted to immerse himself as a ritual step toward responsible membership. He was admitted to the holy water, which may mean not only the ritual baths but the liquid food used by the monks.[171]

Once fully admitted to the community, the new monk was required to follow the *Rule of the Community* in every way. As has been noted, the immersions were frequent because so many incidental matters could quickly render one impure. So the *mikveh* became a significantly important key to the ritual purity of the group.

The Jewish historian, Josephus, gave his own understanding of the Essenes, whom he broke into two divisions. Josephus' accuracy, however, is not entirely

---

[169] John Allegro. ibid.

[170] ibid.

[171] Lawrence H. Schiffman. op. cit. pp. 103–104.

reliable. "On occasion, Josephus's *halachic* rulings are incorrect."[172] Rabbi Reznick notes that the one grouping appears to be like the Qumranites. Rabbi Leibel Reznick, in his book, *The Holy Temple Revisited* cites Josephus, also known as Yoseph ben Gurion, regarding the Essenes:

> Before sunrise no one utters a word regarding secular affairs. In prayer they beseech God to make Himself known. Afterwards, they engage in crafts for which they have a reputation. At the fifth hour they bathe in cold water, put on their sacred garments and assemble in a private hall. No one is allowed to enter the hall except the initiated.

> One who desires to join the sect must remain an outsider for one year. During that time he must abide by the rules. He is given a hatchet, a loin cloth, and a set of white garments. When he has shown his temperance, he is admitted closer into the fold, sharing in the waters of sanctification, but cannot participate in the meetings. Only after two years, if he has demonstrated his strength of character and determination, then he is admitted into the society.[173]

> They are divided into four classes according to their training. If a senior member is touched by an inferior member, the senior must immerse himself in a *mikveh* as though he were contaminated by a heathen.[174]

Josephus, however, did not lump all the Essene eggs in one basket. He referred to them as many in every community. He added:

---

[172] Rabbi Leibel Reznick. op. cit., p. 167.

[173] Rabbi Leibel Reznick. op cit.,, p. 165.

[174] Rabbi Leibel Reznick. op. cit., p. 166.

There is a second order of Essenes which agrees with the way of life, customs, and regulations of the first. They differ only with their view of marriage. Marriage, according to them, is a most sacred duty, for without it, the race would disappear. A bride to be is put on three years' probation. They have no intercourse during pregnancy to show that marriage is not for pleasure but to propagate the race. When women immerse themselves, they wear a dress just as the men wear a loincloth. Such are the customs of this order.[175]

The rules of the community make quite clear that theirs is a community of repentance and holiness. Unless the person entering the *mikveh* is conscious of needing forgiveness, the *tevilah* is a waste of his time as this chapter noted earlier.

He shall neither be purified by atonement, nor cleansed by purifying waters, nor sanctified by seas and rivers, nor washed clean with any ablution. Unclean, unclean he shall be. For as long as he despises the precepts of God, he shall receive no instruction in the Community of His counsel."[176]

Yigael Yadin made a similar comment:

The basic difference between the concept of the *mikveh* in traditional Judaism and the *mikveh* . . . with the Essenes and with John – the *mikveh* in normative Judaism was a ritual purity in that sense that it had to do also with physical ritual dirt. If you touched something which was not clean or you did something which was

---

[175] Ibid.

[176] G. Vermes, op. cit., pp. 74, 75; Marcel Simon. op. cit., pp. 75,76.

not clean ritually, several times a day you had to baptize yourself . . .

The Essenes in particular, and John . . . developed [the concept] that you really can't purify your soul with baptism . . . unless you are really just [or] you are pure. It was against this physical use [of] the *mikveh* to get rid of the physical dirt that was the basic difference, I think, between the Essene use of the *mikveh* as we find them at Qumran and the normal *mikveh* in Judaism."[177]

Interestingly, some writers refer to the close connection between the baptism practised in Qumran and Christian baptism. The followers of the "Teacher of Righteousness" at Qumran called themselves "God's elect." Their religious community was the "New Covenant." "Members of the New Covenant were initiated through baptism."[178] The Community Rule, noted Vermes in referring to the *Damascus Document* of the Qumranites, "refers to a purificatory rite in connexion with entry into the Covenant. This seems to have been a particular and solemn act similar to Christian baptism and to have symbolized purification by the 'spirit of holiness.'"[179]

From the same Rule it may be deduced that this 'baptism' was to take place 'in seas and rivers' (111) like the baptism of John and Jesus, and that true conversion was the absolute condition for the efficacy of the sacrament (v). It may be of interest to note that this rite was the baptism administered to proselytes; in the case

---

[177] Paradox: Born King – Interview with Yigael Yadin, op. cit.

[178] Max I. Dimont. op. cit., p. 132.

[179] G. Vermes. op. cit., p. 45.

of women it was the only ceremony of entry into the Covenant of Israel.[180]

Women, however, were not likely to have been a part of the New Covenant of Qumran. Yigael Yadin, in trying to interpret the Temple Scroll, indicates that the future holy city anticipated by the Qumran sect would allow no one but the completely celibate. Since the Qumranites were anticipating such an eschatological city of God, they also tried to model their own community on what they expected of the future one – and differed from the *Oral Torah* and later Rabbinic teachings on exclusivity.[181]

3. Ritual Washing at Masada

The community at Qumran came to a rapid end in AD 66 when hostilities broke out between Rome and its subjects, the Jews. The Qumranites hurriedly hid their precious scrolls from the scriptorium, placing them in the caves made famous in 1947 when the first scrolls were recovered. Undoubtedly, some of the zealots who captured Masada, a few miles south, were part of the Qumranites who had escaped there. The ultimate war was part of their theology and it appeared to some of them that the strife had begun. While they held off the Roman Tenth Legion for almost three years, the observant among them kept faithful to their ritual washings.

Masada fell to a raiding party of the zealots in 66 AD. Their captain, Menachen Ben Yehuda was from Galilee. His

---

[180] Ibid.

[181] Yigael Yadin. The Temple Scroll, pp. 172 – 174.

foray marked the start of the Jewish rebellion against Rome.[182]

Consequently, hundreds of refugees fled to Masada, probably including some of the Qumranites. Eleazar ben-Yair, commander of the fortress, led a kosher community. He created accommodation out of Herod's buildings and raided the supplies which Herod had stored in this escape villa he had created for himself. Eleazar then built workshops in which pottery and cooking vessels were created. He also provided for any religious needs of the refugees.

One such desperate religious need for an Essene zealot was to purify himself for the final conflict, hence the need for a *mikveh*. The insights which Father Danielou stated earlier in this chapter are worth recounting, "The idea that one should prepare himself for the end of the world by doing penance is a familiar one in the Qumran scrolls . . . One cannot help but be struck by the importance that ritual ablutions have for the sectarians of Qumran."[183] That importance carried forward to those who escaped Qumran and joined the zealots of Masada.

Quoting Eleazar, an early pamphlet of Israel's National Parks Authority stated: "For from olden times, we have undertaken to serve neither the Romans nor any other Lords, except God only, for He alone rules over man in truth and justice."[184]

---

[182] Micha Livneh and Ze'ev Meshel. Masada. Pamphlet published by the National Parks Authority. 1965, p. 12.

[183] Jean Danielou. op. cit. p. 22.

[184] Micha Livneh and Ze'ev Meshel. op cit. p. 12.

National and religious zeal had become one in the zealot mind. It was this cast of mind which had made them isolate themselves in Masada. To organize their religious life was essential to them, and they went to great pains to set up the minimum arrangements to provide for religious needs: a synagogue and ritual baths. A large public hall built against the wall was found suitable for a synagogue after some structural changes: as luck would have it, it faced Jerusalem. Two parts of the *Torah* scrolls which were kept there have been found concealed under the floor of the back room. The ritual baths were put up in less pretentious locations; One in a casemate in the southern wall, and another in the courtyard of the building behind the storerooms. Even here, in the middle of the desert, there was no relaxation of the ritual rules, and a particular effort was made to impound rainwater that had not been drawn from a well or cistern, as the *halachah* requires.

Another public religious institution apparently established by the zealots was a *beth midrash* or house of study: they arranged stone benches along the walls and in the centre of a large hall, so as to turn it into a suitable meeting place for the sages and their disciples. Even in Masada, *Torah* study went on. Services were conducted by the priests (*Kohanim*) and Levites, whose status was recognized and preserved at Masada. The "coupons" for their rations are marked *ma'asas kohen* (Priest's tithe) in acknowledgment of the commandment of tithing. "t" for *truma* (gift offering) or "t" for *tevel* (untithed produce). Special rations were allocated for ritual purposes, as evidenced by appropriate inscriptions on the jars: *kodesh* (Holy), "*Ksherin letohorat hakodesh*" (clean for the purposes of Holiness). The zealots had brought Bible scrolls with them to Masada, some of which have been found during the excavations: Genesis, Leviticus, Deuteronomy, Ezechiel (sic) and Psalms. Their sacred writings even included such apocrypha as Ben-Sirah and Jubilees.

Among the refugees at Masada were also Essenes, who brought their own sectarian literature such as the "Song of the Sabbath Sacrifices." Men of different sects and beliefs also found themselves able to live together because of the circumstances and of a common purpose and motivation. The uncompromising desire for freedom united them all for the last fight.[185]

The excavator of Masada, Yigael Yadin, happily reported that on top of the mesa called Masada, the excavators had found a *mikveh* [see cover photo].

> The news that we had brought to light a *mikveh* from the period of the Second Temple quickly spread throughout the country, arousing particular interest in orthodox religious quarters and Talmudic scholars; for the traditional laws of the Talmud relating to the ritual bath are quite complex, and no *mikveh* has so far [1966] been discovered belonging to this very period, the period when so much of the traditional law governing the *mikveh* was written and enacted.[186]

The announcement that the first *mikveh* had been found by Yadin's archaeologists led to an interesting conclusion. Two *mikveh* experts – Rabbis David Muntzberg and Eliezer Alter – and a company of their Hasidic followers climbed the snake path to the top of the mesa of Masada to inspect the discovery. It was their only quest.[187] Later, other *mikve'ot*

---

[185] Ibid.

[186] Yigael Yadin. Masada: Herod's Fortress and the Zealots' Last Stand. p. 165.

[187] Yigael Yadin. Masada: Herod's Fortress and the Zealot's Last Stand, p. 166.

were discovered also atop Masada. However, at the time, this discovery was the first ritual bath unearthed in modern Israel. This was exceedingly important to the rabbinate. No orthodox Jew could dwell in a community without a proper *mikveh*. This one had all the conditions and requirements of a conforming *mikveh*. Yadin commented:

> I confess that during Rabbi Muntzberg's examination I was rather anxious. What would be his finding? His face throughout bore a serious expression, and at times he furrowed his brows as if in doubt as to whether the bath was *kosher*. But when he completed his meticulous study, he announced with beaming face and to the delight of all, that this *mikveh* was indeed a ritual bath "among the finest of the finest, seven times seven."[188]

Aryeh Kaplan, noting the rabbi's authentication of the Masada *mikveh*, concluded, "In the eighteen hundred years that have passed, neither the *mikveh* nor its importance has changed."[189]

---

[188] Ibid.

[189] Aryeh Kaplan. op. cit., p. 3.

CHAPTER 3

Excavations at the Ophel

The so-called "Six-Day War" of June, 1967 changed many conceptions about the archaeological structures of Jerusalem. For the first time since the Romans left their governed province of Palestina, archaeologists were free to explore many facets of Israel that were previously out-of-bounds for them.

The archaeologists still had limitations. Religious and/or political influences from both Jewish Orthodoxy and Muslim clerics, the Waqf, (Muslim Council) continued to prevent them from uprooting the grounds on the Temple Mount. For Orthodox Jews, treading on what might have been the location of the Holy of Holies is anathema. For Muslim clerics, the site is considered holy because of the Moslem tradition that their prophet, Mohammed, ascended from this Mount for a night visitation in heaven.

The Temple Mount is further revered because biblical tradition holds that here Abraham met Melchizedek and offered him a tithe while breaking bread and drinking wine together.[190] Moreover, the site commemorates the occasion in which Abraham offered his son as a sacrifice but God intervened by providing a ram.[191] (To the Jews, this son was Isaac; to the Muslims, he was Ishmael).

---

[190] Genesis 14:18.

[191] Genesis 22:13; Hebrews 11:17–19.

Archaeologist Matty Zohar expressed his delight to this writer about the new opportunities which awaited his profession outside the Temple Mount itself.

> The excavations that we have been doing here for the last 13 or 14 years [i.e., 1967, 1968] are very much . . . [different] than what has been done in the last 100 years. Jerusalem is the site that has attracted scholars over the past 100 years and [the most] they could accomplish was [to dig] little holes somewhere.
>
> Warren was the first one to make a very thorough survey of the city of Jerusalem, especially the area surrounding the Temple Mount. He spent most of his time underground in little holes and little water shafts and very valuable information was gathered.
>
> But in 1967, when this part [the Ophel] became part of Israel, we found "happily" that the Jewish Quarter was completely in ruins. We had some dilapidated buildings near here [the Jewish Quarter and near Robinson's Arch]. This gave us, for the first time in the history of archaeology of Jerusalem, [opportunity] to expose not only a small hole or a small section or a water shaft but to expose a whole house or a whole section, or in our case [here], we can see a whole quarter of the city.
> We could now answer some questions which no one previously had tried asking them! What is the relation between private homes and streets? What is the relation between the Temple, which was always the focus of attention of Jerusalem with its surroundings? What was the 'life-setting? How did the people live?[192]

---

[192] Matty Zohar. <u>Paradox: Born King</u>, CTV Toronto Television Documentary, filmed November, 1981.

1. The Jerusalem Holyland Model

The new excavations around Jerusalem, including some hints at what the Ophel looked like in Jesus' time, resulted in a model – on a 1:50 scale – of Herodian Jerusalem. It covers several hundred square metres. It was constructed at the Holyland Hotel in Jerusalem and was based on data supplied by Professor M. Avi Yonah. The data derive from texts, such as Josephus, and from the archaeological information. The model is less than perfect. The Temple depiction is fairly accurate, but other placements may not be correct. As Father Jerome Murphy-O'Connor suggests, "imagination often supplied what the texts or archaeological trowel did not supply."[193]

Consequently the depictions of the arrangements at the model showing the Ophel are somewhat inaccurate. The Antonia may be too large. The model shows a number of houses leading up to the entrance Triple *Hulda* Gates, and one central building which was used for the Jews' ritual washings, the passport to the Temple itself. It shows only two entrance gates for the *Hulda* Gates when actually there were three. The exit (Double) *Hulda* Gates were indeed two in number. Moreover, the public *mikveh* building must have been considerably larger in order to accommodate the crowds of men seeking entrance to the Temple. Possibly, there were more such public buildings than one. As was noted by Ben-Dov, many of the Ophel's private houses also had *mikve'ot* as part of their "rental appeal."

With new information now available, a reconstruction of the Holyland Model of Herodian Jerusalem is in order and

---

[193] Murphy-O'Connor, Jerome. op. cit., p. 144.

overdue. However slightly incorrect the model may be, it serves a helpful purpose.

2. The Hulda Gates and Tunnels

Three sets of apparent entrances to the gates can still be found by an observer visiting the Ophel in Jerusalem today. They are known as the *Hulda* (var. *Chulda*, *Huldah*) Gates. "The word *Hulda* in Hebrew means weasel or mole (Lev. 11:29), a name perhaps suggested by the tunnel-like passage up to the Temple courts."[194] *Hulda* also is the name of a prophetess (2 Kings 22:14; 2 Chronicles 34:22). One gate is single, one triple and one double. The Double Gate served for both exits and entrances.

> [It] was one of the southern entrances into the Court of the Gentiles in Herodian times. There is a massive lintel stone above the arch and other large stones along the side, all of which are Herodian. Behind the gate entrance is a double-vaulted vestibule which leads into an ascending passageway under the present al-Aqsa [var. El Aqsa] Mosque, coming out of the east of the mosque. Both passageway and vestibule show Herodian masonry.

Kathleen Kenyon's discoveries were only partial. More work has been done since then. The dating of her work and that of others is sometimes clouded by dating definitions. She wrote that she uses "the term 'Herodian' for the period of Herod the Great. Professor Mazar used it more generally

---

[194] W. Harold Mare. The Archaeology of Jerusalem, p. 153 footnote.

for the whole period down to the destruction in AD 70."[195] She noted those differences of dating in writing of excavations at the *Hulda* Gates.

> The south wall of the Haram [*Harem el Sharif*, the Temple Mount platform] provides evidence of two ancient gates, the Double Gate and the Triple Gate. The paving of the street running along the south wall of the Haram has largely been robbed towards the east, but it is clear that the street was leading to the Double Gate. Excavations in this area are proceeding apace. I can only record my 1972 appreciation of the results. This appreciation was that the street along the southern wall provided access to the Double Gate and the Triple Gate. Each of these gates was also approached by steps from the south. At this point I must make a reservation concerning Mazar's interpretation. Excavation in such terribly complicated areas of successive destruction, building stages, and occupational levels requires a detailed and very patient excavation technique that he did not employ. There is no doubt that associated with Herod's building operations there was quarrying on a large scale in the whole area to the south of the Haram. I think that the evidence suggests that all the rock-cuttings adjacent to the revealed stairs belong to an earlier period, and are not associated with the Herodian temple.[196]

Rabbi Leibel Reznick likewise commented on the dating of the gates and their purposes.

> Today there are six gateways built into the [southern] wall. Facing the wall, starting from the right, is a single

---

[195] Kathleen Kenyon. Digging Up Jerusalem, p. 221 footnote.

[196] Kathleen Kenyon. op. cit., p. 228.

arched doorway called the Single Gate. Next to it are three arched gateways called the Triple Gates. To the left is a double arched gateway called the Double Gate. All were built at least a thousand years after the destruction of the Temple. All have been sealed up with stone walls. A Crusader tower was built next to the Southern Wall; it completely covers the left Double Gate and blocks half the view of the right Double Gate. Although no remains of the *Chulda* [*Hulda, Huldah*] Gates are to be found, there are telltale signs that mark their exact location.

The Single Gate was built entirely of smaller stones. Not a single Herodian ashlar was used in its construction. It was built by the Crusaders around the year 1100 and was used as an entrance into the lower Temple complex.

The Triple Gate, however, does contain a Herodian stone at the base of the left doorpost. The question has been posed as to whether this is the location of some Temple Gate or if this gateway, like the Single Gate, is of later construction. When Herod had Temple gateways built, the right and left gateposts had decorative molding carved on the outside. On the Triple Gate, the Herodian stone at the bottom of the far left doorpost still has this decorative molding. This indicates that it is the Temple gate. We can now at least place the left doorpost on one of the *Chulda* Gates. But was the *Chulda* Gate a large single gate, a double gate or even a triple gate similar to the one that is there today?

The Double Gate contains a sign of the presence of a Temple gate. As mentioned earlier, most of the Double Gate is blocked by the Crusader tower. On a small portion that is exposed are the remains of a Byzantine cornicestone. An important feature of Herodian architecture was to be seen above the lintel-stone. A series of stones, forming a small arch, spanned the lintel. Above the Byzantine cornice, part of this Herodian arch can be seen, indicating another Temple gate.

In the time of the Temple, these doorways led to anterooms, which in turn led to the *Chulda* Tunnels; they are still there today. In centuries past, they, too, were used as mosques called *El Kadimah*."[197]

3. Unearthing *Mikve'ot*

The discovery of a *mikveh* at Masada, as well as at the Herodium, and the *mikve'ot* at Qumran have alerted archaeologists that other ritual baths might be found throughout Israel. Nazareth's St. Joseph's church contains an ancient *mikveh*. An earlier discovery of a *mikveh* in the Essene Quarter on Mount Zion early in the 20th century proved that the immersion sites had already existed in Jerusalem. Since the unearthing of *mikve'ot* at the Ophel from excavations since 1967, more *mikve'ot* were also unearthed in the former Essene Quarter.[198] These ritual immersion vats were deemed exceedingly important for the ritual purity of Essenes and observant Jews.

Since the new political situation of 1967, and to the delight of "diggers" and *Torah* and *Talmud* scholars, many more *mikve'ot* were uncovered at the Ophel. Matty Zohar explained:

In [front of] the main entrance [the Triple Hulda Gates] of the two ways to get into the Temple we have a very broad staircase [where also] we have an enormous system of accumulation of water holes. They served for the *tevilah*, for the purification. Whenever anyone wanted to enter the temple, he had to be ritually clean. He [could] do this in only one spot – at the southern

---

[197] Rabbi Leibel Reznick. The Holy Temple Revisited, pp. 42–44.

[198] James Charlesworth. Jesus and the Dead Sea Scrolls. New York: Doubleday, 1992. p. 213.

wall. We know of some more entrances on the Temple Mount, for the priests and for others. They could do their rituals on the Temple Mount itself. The people [who were not clerics] had to do this outside the Temple Mount before they could go into the Temple Mount. So, for the people, there was only one entrance where they could go in, where for the others there were many more. The idea was that you [the Romans and the High Priest's Security Force] could easily confine the people so that you could control them. When you have several other entrances you cannot control them.[199]

The small entrance passage to the Temple Mount obviously served a double purpose. It permitted worshippers to attend the sacrificial activities of the Temple cult, ensuring that each one of them had been suitable ritually prepared for the rites of sacrifice. It likewise served to keep control of the people. The Roman soldiers were not permitted to enter the Temple Mount, so the Ophel was their main control station. Likewise, since entrance to the Temple Mount itself (save for the Court of the Gentiles) could include no Gentiles, it protected the interests of Temple defilement. Gentiles may have been permitted to enter the Court of the Gentiles, however, through the Double Gate, mostly an exit from the Temple Mount, where a series of tunnels allowed them access.

Joachim Jeremias noted some non-Jews, pilgrim caravans also attended the festivals from the Diaspora, surely coming to Jerusalem as God-fearers. They participated in some aspects of the feast days.[200]

---

[199] Matty Zohar. op. cit.

[200] Joachim Jeremias. Jerusalem in the Time of Jesus, p. 77.

The full proselyte was bound to make the pilgrimage (cf. Gal. 5:3 where Paul cites the Jewish regulations). But more than once we also come across so-called 'God-fearers' at the festivals in Jerusalem: 'Now there were certain Greeks among those who went up to worship at the feast' (John 12:20): these were the uncircumcised "God-fearers,' as was the treasurer of the Ethiopian Candace (Acts 8:28ff.). Josephus in BJ 6.427, mentions 'any foreigners present for worship.' In such cases the people were no doubt taking part of their own free will. In 1871 C. S. Clermont-Ganneau found a Greek inscription near what would have been the sanctuary with these words: "No foreigner is to enter within the balustrade and the embankment that goes around the sanctuary. If anyone is caught in the act, he must know that he has himself to blame for the penalty of death which will follow."[201]

Indeed, that may have been the High Priest's control centre when Paul was accused of bringing at Gentile into the Temple, upon his return to Jerusalem to fulfil a vow.[202] The Temple watchmen dragged Paul from the Temple Mount itself so that they would not spill his blood and defile the Temple. Then the Jewish "police" dragged him through the exit tunnel and emerged through the Double Gate where Roman soldiers were permitted.

A cohort was handy when Paul was thus dragged to be beaten and prevented further harm to him.[203] Paul was then

---

[201] T. C. Smith. The Broadman Bible Commentary. Acts, Vol. 10., p. 124.

[202] Acts 21:26–28.

[203] Acts 21:30–33.

removed to the "barracks," i.e., the Antonia, or Praetorium, where the tribune, Claudius Lysias permitted Paul to address the gathering crowd.[204]

What else does the writer of Acts mean in saying Paul purified himself, than that he used the *mikveh* for ceremonial washing prior to entering the temple? Such immersion was obligatory. Paul remained loyal to the *Oral Torah* even though he knew his righteousness was not earned but came to him by the grace of God. And where else would Paul purify himself other than at the Ophel?

Avigad reported that the ritual baths are the most frequently found in all the houses of the Upper City of Jerusalem. "At least one and most often two or more ritual baths existed in every house, attesting to the strict observance of the laws of ritual purity."[205] He also reported, that unlike the house *mikve'ot* unearthed below the Temple Mount at the Ophel, or at Masada, the Upper City houses had no "treasury" (*otzar*). He suggests that the householders found a different way to "purify" the *mikveh* water.[206] He noted that two especially large ritual baths uncovered in the Great Mansion of the Upper City had two doorways, side by side.

> The bather could enter through one doorway before purification and exit ritually purified after immersion through the other (*Mishnah*, Shekalim 8:2). Sometimes the two paths – descending into the pool and ascending

---

[204] Acts 21:37–40.

[205] Nahman Avigad. The Herodian Quarter in Jerusalem, p. 19.

[206] Ibid.

from it – were divided down the middle of the steps by a low partition.[207]

The discovery of such a large number of *mikve'ot* in the Ophel surprised even the archaeologists.[208] The details of the *mikve'ot* were in keeping with the conventions described in the *Mishna(h)* many years later. Meir Ben-Dov describes what his team uncovered.[209]

The ritual baths were coated with a grey-coloured plaster to prevent seepage. In addition to the lime and sand – the standard ingredients of the plaster – olive oil was added to strengthen it and enhance its impermeability. The ritual bath was entered by at least six steps that were covered water and were considered to be an integral part of the bath. Anyone who entered the *mikveh* would descend these steps impure and ascend them cleansed. To ensure that the purified bather would not come into contact with the part of the step he had tread while descending into the *mikveh*, a number of baths had railings to divide the steps and indicate one side for descent and the other for ascent (we have evidence of this convention in the *Mishna*). We also uncovered other kinds of ritual baths within the residential quarters, including "seeded" baths that did not draw upon a "treasury and baths cut into the rocks like caves.[210]

---

[207] Ibid.

[208] Meyer Ben-Dov. op. cit. p. 152

[209] Meir Ben-Dov. op. cit., p. 152.

[210] Ibid.

Ben-Dov described the covering over the *mikve'ot* as having vaulted roofs.[211] Since those males using the *mikve'ot* needed to bathe themselves while naked, the vaulted coverings provided a measure of modesty to the adherents of the Temple sacrificial cult.

This profusion of ritual bathing vats indicated the large influx of pilgrims who came to the Temple as was their spiritual obligation. They had brought an offering, and to present it atop the Temple Mount, the pilgrims first had to ensure their righteousness according to the laws of *tevilah*. This discussion is expanded in chapter 6 of this book.

In Jerusalem, during Herodian times, provision was made for those foreign pilgrims entering the Temple Mount to prepare themselves ritually for the sacrifices. By Herodian times, Jews had scattered for a variety of reasons – economics, persecution, personal preference – throughout the Graeco-Roman world. Often, they pursued occupations which permitted them to honour the *kosher* admonitions. These same occupations, such as textiles and banking, allowed them to avoid the workers guilds' pagan practices of patron deity worship.

Many observant Jews who lived abroad and who had taken on Hellenistic habits and characteristics, remembered the LORD's injunction "Three times a year you are to celebrate a festival to me."[212] The injunction included that the worshippers should not come "empty-handed" when they came to worship God.[213] A sacrifice was as appropriate as their presence. So they travelled to Jerusalem to honour the

---

[211] Ibid.

[212] Exodus 23:14.

[213] Exodus 23:15.

command and to renew their Jewish sensibilities. Many also came for business reasons – what an opportunity to network!

These holy days were the Feast of Unleavened Bread (*pesach*, Passover), The Feast of Harvest (*shavuot*, First Fruits, Pentecost) and the Feast of Ingathering (*succoth, Booths, Tabernacles*). Increased attendance at the Temple Mount reflected the seasonal pilgrimages made by Jews living outside Roman Palestina. Evidence of the swollen attendance at *Shavuot* is reflected by the exceedingly large number of persons listening to Peter's address there.[214] The writer of Acts indicates they were together in one place.

The only plausible place to accommodate these thousands of pilgrims was at the Ophel below the southern rim of the Temple Mount, where they would have taken turns for *tevilah*. The list of visitors to Jerusalem is significant. They included a variety of origins from Rome to North Africa, from present day Turkey to Mesopotamia, from Egypt to Crete – and from a smattering of other points on the atlas. The number responding positively to Peter's invitation to accept Jesus as their saving Messiah and LORD was three thousand who were appropriately baptized (not just ritually washed or ritually immersed) and "added to their (the followers of Jesus) number that day."[215]

The differences between *tevilah* and the initial Christian baptisms were dramatic. The immersion vats were used only to accommodate those pilgrims coming for self-immersion. Second Temple Judaism knew nothing except self-immersion. An administrator of baptism was not only unorthodox but likely would invalidate the pilgrim's ritual

---

[214] Acts 2;1 ff.

[215] Acts 2:41.

immersion. What was permitted was an observer to ensure that the individual was totally immersed – every hair and body fold.

Modern "Messianic" Jews reject outright any notion of an agent in Christian baptism. Peter's sermon[216] admonition to "be baptized" (not baptize themselves) "in the name of Jesus," argue Messianic Jews, violated the individual nature of those being baptized by advocating an administrator and the rationale for immersion. No doubt, many who were present on Pentecost 1, would have thought so too.

Yet, the place of immersion is both a tomb and a womb. One cannot bury himself; someone else must do it for him. Similarly, if the place of baptism is a womb, someone must act as a midwife. An agent had a symbolic role to play.

As we shall see in subsequent chapters, effectively, the administration represented a priestly function, an initiation symbolic of one's dependence upon God's grace for salvation and fellowship with God. Similarly, the baptism "in the name of Jesus" symbolized the death and resurrection of Jesus, the new way[217] to the Father in heaven, the new *halaka* for those who wanted to be right and walk with God.

---

[216] Acts 2

[217] John 14:6; Acts 9:2; Acts 16:17; Acts 18:26.

Part Two: Christian Baptism

CHAPTER 4

John the Baptist and Baptism
Repentance, Initiation and Commitment

Some 40 years before the Qumran community collapsed, John the Baptist had begun his ministry of preaching and baptizing at the River Jordan. His activity was a cause of concern to many, as John's Gospel attests: "Now a discussion about purification arose between John's disciples and a Jew."[218]

1. Who Was John the Baptist?

The Bible relates that John, dubbed "the Baptist," was the child of a priest named Zechariah and his wife, Elizabeth.[219] Both had priestly ancestors. Elizabeth traced her ancestry back to Aaron[220] and Zechariah, also a Levite, back through David's division of the Levites into 24 divisions,[221] descending from Abijah. John, therefore, was also of the Levite tribe and in the priestly line but his role

---

[218] John 3:25.

[219] Luke 1:5 ff

[220] Luke 1:5

[221] 1 Chronicles 24 ff.

was prophetic.[222]   His name in Hebrew, *Yohanan*, means "Yahweh has shown favour."[223]

Jesus certainly called him a prophet.[224] Leonard Badia reminds us that the word for prophet is *nabi*[225] which means "to call" or "speak aloud," i.e., "to forthtell," as over against "to foretell."

John's ministry began near where his ascetic development was fed – in the wilderness of Judea. Generally, scholars suggest that wilderness was located in the area directly east of the Mount of Olives as the arid terrain descends toward Jericho. The area is not far – northeast – from Qumran. The site where John baptized and preached is not precisely known.[226] The baptisms took place in the Jordan River. Did he remain in one place for his ministry of

---

[222] Ray Summers. Commentary on Luke, p. 27; Badia, Leonard, op. cit., p. 7.

[223] Joseph A. Fitzmyer. The Anchor Bible Vol. 28: The Gospel According to Luke I–IX, p. 325.

[224] Luke 7:26.

[225] Leonard Badia. op cit., p. 7. Badia offers an exhaustive study of John the Baptist and the Qumran Community. For a thorough investigation of their similarities and differences, consult his research.

[226] Marina Jimenez. "Muddying the Waters: Unholy Squabble as Three Sites Stake Claim to Be Location where Jesus Was Baptized." National Post, 03 January 2000, p. A13; Agence France-Presse. "Pilgrims Flock to Site of Christ's Baptism in Jordan." National Post, 08 January 2000, p. A16; Sandro Contenta. "Was Jesus Baptized in Israel or Jordan?" Toronto Star. 27 November 1999, p. A18.

baptism and preaching? Maybe not! John's Gospel says that he was baptizing at Aenon near Salim, "because there was plenty of water."[227]

That reference may suggest the seasonal amount of water in the Jordan River may have been deep enough at one location but perhaps not at another. It also may imply that the mode was immersion, so that John could completely submerge someone – although, as was shown in chapter one, a person could lie prone in a stream for ritual purification and allow the water to run over him or her.

The Gospels hint at a further conflict about the location of John's baptism of Jesus. John says the baptismal place was near Bethany[228] (or Bethabara) on the east bank of Jordan. The Fourth Gospel notes that Jesus came from Galilee for the baptism by John and was with two of his disciples, staying in the area where John was baptizing.[229] It tells also that Jesus decided to leave the "next day" for Galilee.[230]

Matthew, however, inserts the temptation story at this point, suggesting that Jesus stayed in the wilderness area for 40 days longer.[231] The chronologies and the locations are unclear. What seems clear is the contrasting connection of

---

[227] John 3:23.

[228] John 1:28.

[229] John 1:38.

[230] John 1:43.

[231] Matthew 4:1 ff.; Luke 4:1–13.

Jesus to Adam and Eve where the Tempter seduced them, not in a wilderness but in the paradise of Eden.[232]

2. John's Baptism

Since the discovery of the Dead Sea Scrolls, scholars realized that the Essenes built a community at Qumran and imparted a slightly different meaning to ritual immersion than traditional Judaism. Qumran's importance grew immeasurably. Was there a connection, large or small between the Essenes of Qumran and John the Baptist? Indeed, was there a direct connection to Jesus? The latter question is very much in doubt but the connection to John is not so easily dismissed.

In an interview with this writer, Yigael Yadin stated:

> First of all we know that John the Baptist actually roamed about and preached and lived in the same area as Qumran, more or less where the Essenes lived. Secondly, John's preaching about baptism . . . is very similar to what we find actually in the writings of the Essenes. Therefore I think we can't be too wrong in thinking that John was in contact with the Essenes of Qumran. Whether he was an actual member at the time or not that is, of course, a different question. But that he knew them and they knew him, I'm nearly pretty sure about it.[233]

Scholars provide no definitive answer to John's membership in the Qumran sect. At best, students of Qumran believe John and the Essenes may have influenced one another. Both associated immersion with a repentant attitude

---

[232] Genesis 3:6.

[233] Yigael Yadin. personal interview op. cit.

of the candidate. Both anticipated a future personage to right the wrongs of the current social and spiritual situation. For John, it was the one whose sandals he was unworthy to lace. For the Essenes, was it the Teacher of Righteousness? Both held eschatological inclinations in their pronouncements.

Much, however, was different. John appears to have had a special mission, a mission unlike one mission of the Qumranites to replace the priestly illegitimacies of the Jerusalem Temple cult. John's mission was twofold, first to bring people to repentance before God and secondly to baptize those repenting as a shared symbol of their very public confession of sin. John's baptisms were conducted in the face of his sense of imminent judgment.[234] Thirdly, the Scriptures also describe him as the forerunner or herald of Messiah.[235] John himself claimed he came to the place of baptisms to reveal the Lamb of God to Israel.[236]

Consider the differences. John worked primarily alone but eventually with his own set of followers. The Qumranites worked in mutuality, under a leader with authority. The Qumranites allowed only their own community members to use their immersion facilities and then only if they had demonstrated their commitment and loyalty.

John invited people of all races and occupations – Gentiles, tax collectors and soldiers included – to declare by public baptism that they repented of their sins and intended that repentance to make a difference in how they lived. Qumran was a closed society, their rules served to keep

---

[234] Luke 3: 7–9.

[235] Mark 1:2; Isaiah 42:1–9; Isaiah 40:3.

[236] John 1:31.

people out; John's attitude was openness. The immersion rituals of traditional Judaism and of the Qumranites were self-administered. The baptism of John included an agent. The Qumranites immersed themselves once or more each day. John seemed to baptize one time only.

Those baptized by John sought his advice:

And the crowds asked him, "What should we do?" In reply he said to them, "Whoever has two coats must share with anyone who has none; and whoever has food must do likewise." Even tax collectors came to be baptized, and they asked him, "Teacher, what should we do?" He said to them, "Collect no more than the amount prescribed for you." Soldiers also asked him, "And we, what should we do?" He said to them, "Do not extort money from anyone by threats or false accusation, and be satisfied with your wages."[237]

John's baptism is clearly described as a "baptism of repentance."[238] He publicly invited anyone to join him in the River Jordan so that by their public demonstration of baptism they could renounce their sins against God and others.[239] Among the people appearing to submit to John's baptism, one figure was different. It was Jesus. John declared

---

[237] Luke 3:10–14.

[238] John 3:11; Mark 1:4; Luke 3:7, 12; 7:29; Acts 10:27; 13:24; 18:25; 19:3,4.

[239] Luke 3:7–18.

him to be the One who was expected,[240] i.e., Messiah. He also declared him to have no need for baptism.[241]

3. Who Was Jesus?

The birth narratives in two of the Gospels record the genealogy of Jesus. Luke relates that Jesus descended through Joseph, whose forebear was King David.[242] Matthew traces Jesus' ancestry through King David by way of Judah to Abraham.[243]

Matthew's list of Jesus' ancestors left out many of the women in Jesus' descendency but as well as Mary, included four females whose activities and backgrounds are unusual. Tamar was an incestuous person. Rahab was a harlot. Ruth was a Moabitess and therefore a former outsider in the camp of Israel. The fourth "scarlet woman" was Bathsheba, not named but referred to by Matthew as "the wife of Uriah."[244] Since Mary is described in Luke as a relative of Elizabeth,[245] can we conjecture that she therefore derived from Levitical stock? Such a family tie would further connect the concept

---

[240] John 1:29, 35.

[241] Matthew 3:14.

[242] Luke 2:4.

[243] Matthew 1:1 ff.

[244] Matthew 1:6.

[245] Luke 1:36.

that Jesus was the great High Priest,[246] as well as David's Son and Lord.[247]

John's Gospel prologue paints a different description of Jesus. It borrows from Philo's philosophy, adapted from the Stoics,[248] using the concept of the Word (*logos*) to describe Jesus as the principle of reality.

> [Philo] Interpreted the concept in the light of God as Creator; the Logos, like wisdom, was viewed as God's medium of creation and governance of the world and of revelation to the world. As such, the logos is termed the image of God and the First-born Son of God. Since he is the medium through which the world approaches God, he is also termed the High Priest, the Paraclete for the forgiveness of sins and the bestowal of God's blessings on man.[249]

John the Baptist had his own understanding of Jesus' identification. John saw Jesus as someone so above him in spiritual stature that John himself claimed he was not worthy to untie his sandals.[250]

> The next day he saw Jesus coming toward him and declared, Here is the Lamb of God who takes away the sin of the world! This is he of whom I said, After me

---

[246] Hebrews 8:1 ff.

[247] Matthew 22:41–46.

[248] George R. Beasley-Murray. Word Bible Commentary: John, Second Edition, Vol. 36, p. liv.

[249] Ibid.

[250] Matthew 3: 27.

comes a man who ranks ahead of me because he was before me. I myself did not know him; but I came baptizing with water for this reason, that he might be revealed to Israel."[251]

John obviously had some insights into the person of Jesus but he was also bewildered by him. John seemed to know Jesus – was he not a relative? – and yet the Baptist did not fully know him. John was insightful but perplexed. He stated:

After me comes a man who ranks ahead of me because he was before me. I myself did not know him; but I came baptizing with water for this reason, that he might be revealed to Israel. And John testified, I saw the Spirit descending from heaven like a dove, and it remained on him. I myself did not know him, but the one who sent me to baptize with water said to me, He on whom you see the Spirit descend and remain is the one who baptizes with the Holy Spirit. And I myself have seen and have testified that this is the Son of God.[252]

Obviously, the mystery that is Jesus defies absolute definition. He is much more than the descriptive modifiers used by John the Baptist or the Fourth Gospel or even Pauline ascriptions to him. All of Jesus' followers cannot completely grasp his full identity and most are more bewildered by him than John the Baptist. John MacBeath wrote: "After what manner can any of us prepare to write or speak about the Lord? None of us can say the perfect word

---

[251] Matthew 3: 29 ff.

[252] John 3: 31–34.

or the adequate word about him. He surpasses language."[253]
Consider Philip Yancey's words:

> Sometimes I accept Jesus' audacious claim without
> question. Sometimes, I confess, I wonder what
> difference it should make to my life that a man lived two
> thousand years ago in a place called Galilee. Can I
> resolve this inner tension between doubter and lover?[254]

Both doubt and love lingered with John and his
devoted followers. From prison, John sent an envoy with a
serious question for someone unsure of his invested faith.
"Are you the one who was to come, or should we expect
someone else?"[255] Jesus answered, "Blessed is he who does
not fall away because of me."[256] Even when some disciples
said they understood his identity,[257] their doubts persisted.[258]

4. John's Baptism of Jesus

Doubts aside, John immersed Jesus in the Jordan. Each
of the Gospels relates a slightly different version of the
event. Apparently John prepared the crowds at the baptismal
site for Jesus arrival, even though John himself was not fully

---

[253] John MacBeath. <u>The Face of Christ</u>. p. vii.

[254] Philip Yancey. <u>The Jesus I Never Knew</u>. p. 17.

[255] Matthew 11: 3.

[256] Matthew 11: 6.

[257] Matthew 16: 18.

[258] John 13: 21–27; 20: 25.

aware of the identity of the "long-expected" Saviour and Messiah.

> I baptize you with water for repentance, but one who is more powerful than I is coming after me; I am not worthy to carry his sandals. He will baptize you with the Holy Spirit and fire . . . They asked him, Why then are you baptizing if you are neither the Messiah, nor Elijah, nor the prophet? John answered them, I baptize with water. Among you stands one whom you do not know, the one who is coming after me . . . This is he of whom I said, "After me comes a man who ranks ahead of me because he was before me . . ."[259]

So, John baptized Jesus. But what happened here? The baptism seems to be more of an announcement than it does an action of repentance. The reference to the Father's approval[260] turns back to a Messianic Psalm.

> This harks back to Psalm 2. Here the Father speaks of the only begotten Son to whom he will give the heathen for an inheritance. He shall be his "king upon my holy hill of Zion." Though the heathen shall rage and kings shall plot, the Son is promised victory. His victory shall not be military but spiritual. The Jews looked for the former. God gives the latter. He will go through the cross to the throne. Again the thought of sacrifice appears.[261]

As to the matter of repentance, the Scriptures argue that Jesus was sinless and without a blemish. "How much more," asks the writer of Hebrews, "will the blood of Christ, who

---

[259] Matthew 3: 11; John 3: 23 ff.

[260] Matthew 3: 17.

[261] Herschel H. Hobbs. The Gospel of Matthew. p. 26.

through the eternal Spirit offered himself unblemished to God, cleanse our consciences from acts that lead to death, so that we may serve the living God!"[262]

> The baptism acknowledges Jesus as God's Son and Messiah. In Mark this seems to be a personal experience in which Jesus recognizes his true nature: Jesus alone sees "the heavens torn apart" and hears the divine voice proclaiming "You are my Son, the Beloved" (Mark 1: 10–11). In Luke, the proclamation is described as a physical phenomenon: "The Holy Spirit descended upon him in bodily form like a dove" (Luke 3:22). In Matthew, the divine words are spoken in the third person ("This is my Son"), thus addressing the public who stand as witnesses to Jesus' divinity (Matthew 3: 16–17). God's utterance is drawn from Psalm 2:7, and other messianicly interpreted passages from the Hebrew Scriptures, It describes Jesus as the Messiah, God's Son and "Beloved," a word which in Greek can equally mean "Unique One."[263]

Jesus said that he wanted to be baptized by John "to fulfil all righteousness."[264] This may be translated, "We should do all that righteousness demands."[265] "There are two key words in the sentence: To "do all" (literally to "fulfil," the same Greek word Matthew so frequently uses regarding Jesus' fulfilment of Old Testament prophecies) and

---

[262] Hebrews 9:14.

[263] Joshua Roy Porter The Illustrated Guide to the Bible. p. 288.

[264] Matthew 3: 15.

[265] Donald Senior. Invitation to Matthew. p. 45.

"righteousness," or justice. The latter term has a double layer of meaning in biblical thought. God's justice, or righteousness, is the effort we make to respond to God's goodness by carrying out his will."[266]

In addition to his carrying out God's will for him, did that not also mean Jesus was positively identifying himself with the repentant candidates who obediently submitted to the act of repentance in their public baptism? Further is there not an implication that the term "righteousness" was also Jesus' link to the *mikveh* tradition of *tevilah* and all that it implied about becoming a new entity?

The baptism was a signal for many aspects of Jesus' imminent ministry. It was his public introduction, his public pledge, his public affirmation from heaven itself. Moreover, by his immersion in water, he demonstrated his impending death and resurrection. In a way, Jesus by his baptism, simulated the immersion of the high priest (*Kohen Gadol*) entering the Holy of Holies on *Yom Kippur*.

On this most sacred of days, the *Kohen Gadol* would enter the Holy of Holies two times. This, in turn, would require that he change his vestments five times, since he would begin and end with the "golden" ones. Each time before he changed, he would have to immerse himself in a *mikveh*. "The *Kohen Gadol* was not impure or unclean in any way. He was rather undergoing a change in status, symbolized most dramatically by the changes of vestments. When he entered the Holy of Holies, he had a very different status than before – a unique status that would allow him to enter this room. This change in status was achieved through immersion in the *mikveh*.
The immersion in ritual purification involves the very same concept. The water is not washing away any filth.

---

[266] Ibid.

Rather, the *mikveh* is changing the individual's status from that of *tumehomeh* (unclean) to that of *tahor* (clean). Actually, the "purification" is a change of status rather than a "cleansing" process. [267]

We dare to suggest that Jesus would often have used the *mikve'ot* below the Temple Mount. Moreover, he must have done this self-immersion at least three times a year because every observant Jew came to the Temple for the three great feasts of *Pesach*, *Shavuot* and *Succoth*. Jesus said he was observant and came to fulfil the law. [268] But his baptism in Jordan was different from any other ritual immersions in which he may have participated. It was special. His Jordan baptism comprised (1) the announcement of his Messianic identity; (2) the favour he had with his Father; (3) his accepting of those who repented and his solidarity with them; (4) his commitment forward into a ministry; (5) the affirmation of the Holy Spirit and; (6) his death and resurrection.

5. Why an Agent or Administrator in Baptism?

John's baptisms, the baptism by John of Jesus, and any further baptisms mentioned about the early church give a Bible reader pause to ask about an agent or administrator of baptism. No such person existed in the *tevilah* according to Judaism. Part of the answer may lie in the fact that baptism and *tevilah* were not identical. For one thing, repentance for sins was not involved in ritual immersion – except at Qumran. Even among the Qumranites, immersion was self-

---

[267] Aryeh Kaplan. The Waters of Eden. p. 12.

[268] Luke 9: 56.

applied. The Bible nowhere explains this reality and biblical readers are left to speculate on the reasons for a baptismal agent.

Consider possible reasons for an agent. First, an agent represented the action of the Holy Spirit. Self-immersion implies that purification is self-achieved. Employing an administrator / agent suggests that everyone needs a mediator, namely, God's agent, in the forgiveness of sin. Jesus told his disciples how important it was to be trusting.[269] Trust and reliance upon others were the marks of those who were incompetent to achieve their own salvation. An agent implies that the candidate cannot cleanse himself by himself; he or she needs the grace of God to do it.

Secondly, an agent became a visible individual who identified in every way with the candidate. He was a "friend in court" as it were,[270] who joined the candidate and stood with him in the baptismal waters of immersion. This was especially important where those baptized created an ethnic mixture, such as in John's baptism in the Jordan.

Thirdly, everyone needs an agent for burial. The baptistry is a tomb. Who can bury himself? Who indeed!

---

[269] Matthew 18: 4.

[270] Matthew 18:5.

CHAPTER 5

Jesus and Baptism

Rumour declared that Jesus baptized, but fact revealed that Jesus' followers baptized others. "After these things came Jesus and his disciples into the land of Judea; and there he tarried with them, and baptized."[271] The writer of the Fourth Gospel corrected the rumour. "The Pharisees heard that Jesus was gaining and baptizing more disciples than John although in fact it was not Jesus who baptized, but his disciples."[272]

Jesus did not say much about baptism but the few words he declared were especially significant. The first utterance was his own declaration that his baptism was essential for him to fulfil God's will for his life. We have attempted to explain that earlier in the previous chapter.[273] He entered into his own baptism freely and submitted to a human being. He was from God but he submitted to water which was matter. He was master but willing to become a servant. He was pure but he chose to follow God's lead for him to endure the consequence of the sins of the world. This book will attempt to comment on the eloquent example set by Jesus and four other references to baptism, one of them which seems somewhat oblique.

---

[271] John 3:22.

[272] John 4:2.

[273] See chapter 4, section 4.

1. Personal Witness by Example

Although Jesus may have said little about baptism, his few words take on large proportions because of his personal example. The adage "actions speak louder than words" somewhat applies in this situation. Jesus' later words have greater significance because of his own baptism. He led by example. But an example was only a part of his declaration in the Jordan, as was noted in the previous chapter.

George Beasley-Murray writes,[274]

> The opened heaven, the sending of the Spirit and the Voice from the Father all indicate that the last times have dawned, redemption is about to appear. If this be related to the proclamation of John the Baptist, it would be natural to conclude that the Messiah in his baptism is not merely equipped by the Spirit for the work of the Kingdom, but he becomes the "Bearer" of the Spirit, that he might baptize in Spirit and fire.

> The baptism of Jesus takes on a fuller significance from this viewpoint. Far from being a simple acceptance of the death sentence it indicates the initiation of the divine intervention, the downfall of the powers of darkness, the dawn of the new creation, the promise of life from the dead! And this, indeed, is the spirit in which Jesus departed from the Jordan,

Jesus spoke eloquently by the example of his baptism, not only about his Sonship with the Father, but also in the anticipated adoption of all who would soon, by faith, become

---

[274] G. R. Beasley-Murray. Baptism in the New Testament. Grand Rapids MI: William B. Eerdmans Publishing Company, 1962, 1994. p. 61.

children of the Father by their impending belief. By his baptism Jesus enlarged his family.

Beasley-Murray continues:

> Jesus was acknowledged Son of God at baptism (Mk. 1:11) and in him we become sons of God in baptism by faith (Gal. 3:26 ff.). The former citation is a proclamation of the messianic office of Jesus, the latter indicates the creation of a filial relationship to God. There is therefore a vast difference between the two experiences, yet there is also a connection between them. It is because Jesus the Messiah went down to the Jordan to identify himself with the unredeemed, and continued the same process of identification unto the cross and resurrection, that we can share his sonship; that sonship is rooted in the prior filial relation of Jesus to the Father, and the goal of our appropriation of it lies yet in the future, when sonship will be perfected in us (Rom. 8:23; 1 Jn. 3:2). Here again, we see that the baptism of Jesus is critical in the process whereby this goal is achieved, but in a theology of the Incarnation it cannot be viewed as the pattern of Christian baptism. A messianic acknowledgment of the Son by the Father is not the same as the adoption of a sinner by the Father.[275]

2. Water and Spirit

After Jesus' own words at his baptism, the first of the four references is the most oblique of all because it does not use the word "baptism." Jesus said, "I tell you the truth, no one can see the Kingdom of God unless he is born again . . . no one can enter the Kingdom of God unless he is born of water and the Spirit."[276] In the enigmatic conversation Jesus

---

[275] G. R. Beasley-Murray. op. cit. p. 65.

[276] John 3: 3, 5.

had with the Pharisee Nicodemus, he told the Sanhedrin member the "truth" that "no one can enter the Kingdom of God unless he is born of water and the Spirit . . . You should not be surprised at my saying, 'You must be born again.'"[277]

a. Water as Natural Birth

One explanation may be that by mentioning "water" Jesus made no reference to baptism at all. Jesus may have been referring to natural birth, i.e., the amnionic waters. Everyone born into the natural world comes by way of the amnionic sac in which an embryo is protected until "the waters" break at the onset of labour and the child is born. Other commentators say this interpretation is simply a popular viewpoint and "overlooks that the *whole* expression 'of water and Spirit' defines the manner in which one is born from above. Suggestions like these do not do justice to the text and have not commended themselves to scholarly opinion."[278]

Despite Beasley-Murray's dismissal of this interpretation, other scholars sense it may be a good option. Jesus may be saying that a man or woman must be born both physically and spiritually. [279] Wrote Herschel Hobbs, "I see it [water] referring to the natural birth which is accompanied by water. Jesus was endeavouring to lead Nicodemus away

---

[277] John 3: 5–7.

[278] George R. Beasley-Murray. Word Bible Commentary: John, Second Edition, Vol. 36, p. 48.

[279] Thomas D. Lea. "Exegesis of Crucial Texts in John." Southwestern Journal of Theology Volume 31, Fall 1988/ Number 1, p.16.

from the natural to the spiritual birth . . . Jesus definitely contrasted the physical birth and the spiritual birth."[280]

James L. Sullivan concurred. "Jesus' reply . . . seems to use the figure 'born of water' to refer to natural birth, as contrasted with 'born of the Spirit.' It is not enough to be born in the flesh. Men need to be born of the Spirit. To be born only once can be a tragedy. To be born twice is glorious."[281]

b. Water as Regenerator

Thomas D. Lea suggests a second possible reading of this text. "The terms 'water and Spirit' are both describing the word of the Holy Spirit so that Jesus is emphasizing the sovereignty and the divine source of the regenerating work of God."[282] John Polhill adds a comment along this line. "This verse should be seen in the total spectrum of John's use of water imagery. In chapter 4, water will reappear as that life-giving force which comes from within. It is a *symbol* of the new life engendered from within, not the element of an external rite. It is the mysterious work of God's Spirit which is in view, working its renewal imperceptibly from within."[283]

---

[280] Herschel H. Hobbs. The Gospel of John: Invitation to Life. Nashville: Convention Press, 1988, p. 25.

[281] James L. Sullivan. John's Witness to Jesus. Nashville: Convention Press, 1965. p.34.

[282] Thomas D. Lea. op. cit., p. 16.

[283] John B. Polhill. "The Revelation of True Life," Review & Expositor, Vol. 85, No. 3, Summer 1988, pp. 452, 453.

c. Water as Purifier

A third option of interpretation must include "water" as the purifying agent of the ancient *mikveh*. Nicodemus should have understood "water" in this way. "You are a teacher of Israel and you don't understand these things?" asked Jesus of Nicodemus.[284] The Pharisee would have obeyed the *Oral Torah* by immersing himself in a *mikveh* as all observant Jews must have done as required by the obligations of *tevilah*.

Moreover, considering the implications of *tevilah*, the conversation with Jesus fits perfectly in context. In the first chapter of this document this book noted that the *mikveh* simulated the womb and/or tomb and that entering it was akin to death of the former person and in leaving, the egress from the *mikveh* was like a rebirth.[285]

This was the language Jesus used in discussing the Kingdom of God with Nicodemus. Essentially, Jesus was alerting Nicodemus that when God rules one's life, as in the understanding of "the Kingdom of God," it is not enough to go through the automatic rituals of the *mikveh*. One must also be born of the Spirit of God who empowers us to live like God, for God. God's Kingdom requires us to enter his love by physical means and spiritual vulnerability. This is the essence of the *Shema*. "Love the LORD your God with all your heart and with all your soul and with all your strength."[286]

William Barclay stressed this same understanding.

---

[284] John 3: 10.

[285] See Chapter 1.

[286] Deuteronomy 6: 5.

We are born of *water and the Spirit*. There are two thoughts there. *Water* is the symbol of *cleansing*. When Jesus takes possession of our lives, when we love him with all our heart, the sins of the past are forgiven and forgotten. *The Spirit* is the symbol of *power*. When Jesus takes possession of our lives it is not only that the past is forgotten and forgiven; if that were all, we might well proceed to make the same mess of life all over again; but into life there enters this new power which enables us to be what by ourselves we could never do. Water and the Spirit stand for cleansing and the strengthening power of Christ, which wipes out the past and which gives us victory in the future.[287]

Another aspect of this Spirit gift is discussed by William E. Hull.

Jesus readily answered by clarifying that to be born *anew* involved being born of *water and the Spirit*. When the Pharisees had sent representatives to investigate the ministry of John (John 1:19, 24–25), they should have learned that he was baptizing "with water" in anticipation of One who would baptize "with the Holy Spirit" (John 1: 26, 31, 33; cf. Mark 1:8). Now a Pharisee was told that the one whom John promised had arrived – before his very eyes! – and thus the renewal for which John prepared by means of water had become a present possibility through Jesus as bearer of the Spirit (cf. Acts 1:5).[288]

---

[287] William Barclay. The Gospel of John Vol. 1, Edinburgh: The Saint Andrew Press. p. 119.

[288] Hull, William E. The Broadman Bible Commentary, Luke / John, Vol. 9. p. 242.

This dynamic encounter of Jesus and Nicodemus illustrates a similar truth from Jesus recorded by Matthew in response to other Pharisees.

No one sews a patch of unshrunk cloth on an old garment, for the patch will pull away from the garment, making the tear worse. Neither do men pour new wine into old wineskins. If they do, the skins will burst, the wine will run out and the wineskins will be ruined. No, they pour new wine into new wineskins and both are preserved."[289]

This teaching applies to the *mikveh*. The immersion ritual of the *mikveh* is not the medium of purification devised by God's kingdom. God's kingdom uses water as a symbol of new life but only in conjunction with the Spirit's gift of grace. As George A. Buttrick has said, "Christianity made the rite rich in history and more quickening in its significance."[290] Nicodemus cannot be found righteous by his own self-immersion. No one enters God's kingdom by earning the right. Only when the Spirit empowers and sanctifies the penitent can the penitent find entry into God's residence.

The three options of interpretation are not necessarily mutually exclusive. All apply to entry into an eternal existence in God's Kingdom. The new birth requires the unity of heart, soul and strength as the *Shema* commands. God's requirements to enter his Kingdom are his to enunciate.

---

[289] Matthew 9:16–17.

[290] George A. Buttrick. The Interpreter's Bible Volume VII: Matthew. Nashville: Abingdon Press, 1951. p 623.

3. Baptism as Crucible

In Jesus' words about baptism we cannot neglect Jesus' understanding that baptism must never be taken glibly. No doubt those asking for John's baptism of repentance received a degree of offence for their public stand of confession. Watched by the *Torah*-obeying Pharisees, they undoubtedly received ridicule and lack of probation for their courageous stand.

Jesus spoke of an expected baptism of fire through which he would have to pass. When his carefree disciples approached him about favours relating to status and preference in God's Kingdom, he reminded them that service for and to God came at a personal cost.

> I have a baptism to be baptized with, and how am I straitened till it is accomplished!"[291] . . . Jesus said, "Ye know not what ye ask. Are ye able to drink of the cup that I shall drink of, and to be baptized with the baptism that I am baptized with?' They say unto him, 'We are able.' And he saith unto them, 'Ye shall drink indeed of my cup, and be baptized with the baptism that I am baptized with: but to sit on my right hand, and on my left, is not mine to give, but it shall be given to them for whom it is prepared of my Father.'[292]

In this case, Jesus explained that baptism indeed is death to him. The cross is the way to life eternal. To be baptized with Jesus is to enter into his suffering and experience his pain and to offer one's life in full commitment

---

[291] Luke 12: 50.

[292] Matthew 20: 22–23. See also Mark 10: 39.

to God's rule in God's Kingdom. Ray Summers pointed out that

> From the time of his baptism he [Jesus] had identified himself with the Suffering Servant of Isaiah. He saw Israel as an entire people in whose suffering in God's redemptive purpose but narrowing down to one person, in whose suffering that redemptive person would have its realization; he understood that he was that person.[293]

The cross is very much on the horizon for Jesus as he uttered his comments about the cup and baptism. The disciples needed to understand the implications of their association with and endorsement of him. The *koinonia* of the camaraderie was one thing; the *koinonia* (fellowship) of his sufferings was another. Both sides of the discipleship were conjoined and could not be separated.

George R. Beasley-Murray noted,

> The Messiah has both to take the cup of wrath from the hand of God and be plunged beneath the waters of affliction. This he does on behalf of his own and the world . . . fellowship in the sufferings of the Messiah is needful if men would know the fellowship of the Messiah in his Kingdom.[294]

Here baptism is seen as the crucible. The "cup" in Jesus' response and question to his disciples is the one referred to in Psalm 75:8. "In the hand of the LORD is a cup full of foaming wine mixed with spices; he pours it out, and

---

[293] Ray Summers. Commentary on Luke, p. 218.

[294] G. R. Beasley-Murray. Baptism in the New Testament. Grand Rapids MI: William B. Eerdmans Publishing Company, 1962, 1994. p. 75.

the wicked of the earth drink it down to its very dregs." It suggests that sorrow and grief accompany the Suffering Servant's role of serving God and saving his people. Similarly, baptism is a symbol of salvation from God but by way of agony and afflictions. "When you pass through the waters, I will be with you; and when you pass through the rivers, they will not sweep over you."[295]

> A *cup* is to be drunk, a *baptism* is to be endured. The idea of drinking a cup of suffering is frequent in the Old Testament, but significantly it is most often used of the cup of wrath which God apportions to sinful peoples . . . it is natural therefore to understand the parallel figure of baptism in the light of the Old Testament language, wherein sinking beneath the waters symbolizes the experience of overwhelming calamity.[296]

Beasley-Murray also cautions against interpreting Jesus' office as Servant above that of Messiah. He would suffer not only as Servant but as Messiah. "In my judgment it is a questionable procedure that stresses the Servant concept [as Marcus Barth does] in the baptism to the detriment of the Messianic."[297]

The issue is that baptism is no light undertaking. It entails much more than the ritual immersion of *tevilah*. Baptism is a commitment of eternal proportions. Being "buried with Christ in baptism"[298] involves a disciple's deepest connection to the "fellowship of Christ's

---

[295] Isaiah 43: 2.

[296] G. R. Beasley-Murray. op. cit. pp. 73, 74.

[297] G. R. Beasley-Murray. op. cit. p. 50.

[298] Romans 6: 3, 4.

sufferings."[299]   Jesus believed that his disciples lacked understanding of his purpose as Servant and were less than prepared for the total commitment that was expected of both Messiah and his followers.

4. Baptism and Salvation

Jesus made an extraordinary statement about baptism linked with salvation. "He that believeth and is baptized shall be saved; but he that believeth not shall be damned."[300]

First, one must note that some manuscripts – Sinaiticus and Vaticanus – containing this saying do not include Mark 16:9 ff. However, the early church seemed to know of it in the second century and it was quoted by Church Fathers such as Irenaeus and Hippolytus.[301]

Secondly, the emphasis of the saying by Jesus is on "belief" which is followed by baptism. In this sense, baptism was the open declaration of one's belief in Jesus as the crucified and resurrected Saviour, Lord and Messiah. Baptism is the visible declaration of Jesus' death and resurrection as well as the believer's commitment to his Lord.

Baptism links the believer with Jesus' atonement for the believer's sin. It is the sign of release from the bondage of sin. Baptism, by itself is not a factor in salvation but a symbol of its power. The verse is not unlike Paul's report to the Roman church

---

[299] Philippians 3:10.

[300] Mark 16: 16.

[301] D. E. Nineham. The Gospel of Saint Mark. London: Penguin Books, p. 450.

. . . if you confess with your mouth, "Jesus is Lord," and believe in your heart that God raised him from the dead, you will be saved. For it is with your heart that you believe and are justified, and it is with your mouth that you confess and are saved . . . everyone who calls upon the name of the Lord will be saved.[302]

5. Jesus' Charge to Baptize as Part of a Discipling Witness

Jesus' last word on baptism was given as he charged his disciples for their mutual mission. "Therefore go and make disciples of all nations, baptizing them in the name of the Father, and of the Son, and of the Holy Spirit and teaching them to obey everything I have commanded you."[303] The primary verb in this text is "make disciples" (*mathetusate*). The secondary verbs are gerundial, i.e., baptizing (*baptizontes*) and teaching (*didaskontes*).

Interpretation of this section is not without controversy. Beasley-Murray points out how the flow of syntax in the Greek is important for understanding the meaning of Jesus' words.

From the linguistic point of view, Lindblom has pointed out that when participles in Greek are co-ordinated with the main verb they are linked by means of a *kai*, or *te* . . . *kai*, or *dé*: if they follow one another without any such binding conjunction or particle they must be viewed as depending on one another or depending in differing ways on the chief verb. This accords with the situation envisaged in the Commission, that the proclamation of the redemption of Christ should be made and those

---

[302] Romans 10: 9–13.

[303] Matthew 28: 19.

responding in repentance and faith should be baptized and come under instruction. Baptism and instruction do not stand in the same relation to the action of making disciples. The chief action in the main verb is preaching, the plain common sense of which is doubtless the reason for its lack of mention; but the preaching must be received if a hearer is to become a disciple, so the reception of faith is also presupposed in the verb *matheteusate*, "make disciples." It is when a hearer believes and is baptized that he becomes a full disciple; which is the same as saying that a disciple is made such in *baptism by faith* . . . Baptizing belongs to the means by which a disciple is made. The instruction comes after.[304]

Jesus' emphasis, therefore, was that the disciples, in turn, disciplize others. In the process of making disciples they were to baptize the converts and then to instruct them in Jesus' understanding of the Kingdom of God. *Baptism* was the signal of their faith in the crucified and resurrected Saviour. *Learning* was their signal of submission to Jesus' Lordship, God's Kingdom and his rule in their lives.

This writer is perfectly willing to accept Jesus' words in the Great Commission at face value. They adequately reflect what happened at his own baptism where the triune God – Father, Son and Holy Spirit – was reported as affirming Jesus' baptism and its implications. There, the writers reported Jesus' actions and words, the Father's affirmation and blessing together with the Holy Spirit's symbolic presence. Some scholars – indeed many scholars – propose that Matthew's words using the Trinitarian formula at baptism was a late interpolation of Jesus' "last words." Their basic argument is that Matthew (Luke too) probably wrote the Gospel quite late in the first century when the

---

[304] G. R. Beasley-Murray. <u>op. cit</u>. p. 89.

Trinitarian formula was already being used, i.e., as the *Didache*[305] required of converts and catechists. Some attribute the formula to the second century.

Probably it is a moot point. As Frank Stagg noted, the earliest church records in Paul's writings[306] and in Acts[307] indicate that baptisms were in the name of Jesus. He wrote, "It is significant that although a Trinitarian formula is employed, *name* is singular. Although God came to be known as Father, Son and Holy Spirit, he remained one God. *Name* in biblical usage stands for the person himself."[308]

Professor Beasley-Murray offered his opinion on the matter. He also suggested a reason that the importance of baptism is currently downplayed may derive from the scholars' denigration of Jesus' words:

> It has long been an element of critical orthodoxy to regard Mt.28:18–20 as unauthentic, a product of second generation Christianity, reflecting a theology characteristic of the end of that generation rather than its beginning . . . is it not to be wondered at that New Testament scholars have declined to use the Matthean text as evidence of the instruction of our Lord on baptism, or even as shedding light on the origins of

---

[305] David Watson. I Believe in the Church. London: Hodder and Stoughton, 1982, 1985. p. 235.

[306] 1 Corinthians 12:4–6; 2 Corinthians 13:14.

[307] Acts 2:38; 8:16.

[308] Frank Stagg. Broadman Bible Commentary Volume 8: Matthew. Nashville: Broadman Press, 1969. p. 252.

Christian baptism? . . . There are signs of withdrawals from the ranks of the critically orthodox.[309]

In his final instruction[310] to his embryo church, Jesus placed baptism as a very high imperative. It was a disciple's assurance that his or her sins were forgiven by Jesus Christ on the cross. Jesus' church, therefore, must also interpret this order as exceedingly important for its public witness. Baptism in its own right, like Christian teaching, must never exceed the primary importance of making disciples but neither can it be separated from the expression of faith made by a disciple.

---

[309] G. R. Beasley-Murray. op. cit. p. 77.

[310] More will be written of this "Great Commission" in the next chapter.

CHAPTER 6

Christ's Church Embraces Baptism

Obeying Instructions and Employing Symbolism

Jesus gave many instructions. Among them was the charge to his disciples to baptize.[311] The instructions have been dubbed "the Great Commission." Jesus commissioned the eleven disciples present on the authority he had received from the Father. He chose to speak with authority because the scripture records that, "some doubted."

> All authority in heaven and on earth is given to me. Go therefore and make disciples of all nations, baptizing them in the name of the Father and of the Son and of the Holy Spirit, and teaching them to obey everything that I have commanded you. And remember, I am with you always, to the end of the age."[312]

The phrasing in that commission is important. The main verb in Greek is *matheteusate*, "make disciples." The verbs *baptizontes* (baptizing) and *didaskontes* (teaching) are subordinate, supportive and gerundial. Jesus' primary commission to his disciples was to "disciplize," i.e., to win people as Jesus' followers and to help them in the disciplines of Christ's understanding of the "kingdom of God."

---

[311] Matthew 28:19, 20.

[312] Matthew 28:17.

The kingdom of God (or of heaven, *à la* Matthew) is the reality where God rules in the life of those who love him. In this writer's view, the Great Commission was Jesus' version of *halaka*, or walking with God in Jesus' fellowship in the kingdom of God. The supporting verbs, therefore are key aspects endorsing the main task of "disciplizing."

Obviously, making a disciple must occur prior to baptism or teaching, although some preliminary teaching is necessary in the initial stages of making a disciple. The minimum teaching involves how Jesus loves us, who he is, what he did, what he stood for and why we should follow him. The remainder of the teaching element is a lifelong process of learning Jesus' *halaka*, what the first Johannine letter describes in this way:

> If we say we have fellowship with him while we are walking in the darkness, we lie and do not do what is true; but if we walk in the light as he himself is in the light, we have fellowship with one another and the blood of Jesus his (God's) Son cleanses us from all sin.[313]

Making disciples is both a "start-up" challenge in bringing people into the kingdom of God in fellowship with him – evangelism and conversion, if you will – and a lifelong learning experience of growing in God's grace. In writing to the Colossian believers, the Apostle Paul put the second challenge this way:

> For this reason, since the day we heard it, we have not ceased praying for you and asking that you may be filled with the knowledge of his (God's) will in all spiritual wisdom and understanding, so that you may lead lives worthy of the Lord, fully pleasing to him, as you bear

---

[313] 1 John 1:6, 7.

126

fruit in every good work and as you grow in the knowledge of God.[314]

The modifying words of "baptizing" and "teaching" associated with Jesus' final instructions imply the inner and outer expressions of discipleship. A disciple is a learner, hence the emphasis on teaching. Immediately after the events of *Shavuot*, the apostles began the teaching aspect of Jesus' great commission, for Acts reports, "They [the new converts of Pentecost] devoted themselves to the apostles' teaching and to the fellowship, to the breaking of bread and prayer."[315]

"Baptizing in the name of the Father, Son and Holy Spirit" implies identification with Jesus as Saviour, Lord and Messiah. Ritual immersion in traditional Judaism was a physical matter which was deemed to impute righteousness. Baptism in the name of Jesus, or in the name (*not* names) of the Father, Son and Holy Spirit, implied a spiritual identification in which one places allegiance and trust in the Saviour. The loyalty and faith thus demonstrated reflects the disciple's implicit trust in Jesus' death and resurrection as a one-time-for-all atonement of the believer's sin.

The formula, "Father, Son and Holy Spirit" is somewhat disputed by biblical critics. That Matthew wrote it is not often disputed. That Jesus said it is disputed. David Watson, an Anglican priest commented on the issue.

Jesus commanded his followers to 'go and make disciples of all nations, baptizing them in the name of the Father and of the Son and of the Holy

---

[314] Colossians 1:9, 10; see also 1 Thessalonians 2:12.

[315] Acts 2:42.

Spirit' (Matthew 28:19). Yet this passage, too, has been questioned for numerous reasons – textual, literary, historical and theological. However, it fits in well with all that has gone on before in the Gospels and with apostolic practice and teaching in the rest of the New Testament. Further, if it is true, as some maintain, that these words come from the evangelist and not from Jesus and that this Trinitarian baptismal formula was not used by the church until the second century, we are faced with other problems. The words are found in all manuscripts; and it is hard to see why Matthew inserted them if, at the time they formed no part of the church's liturgy. Admittedly the baptisms recorded in Acts were "in the name of the Lord (Jesus)" and not in the name of the Trinity; but these were baptisms for those who already possessed a basic belief in the one true God before they heard the good news of his Son Jesus Christ. Thus baptism in his name was the all-important issue; and it is quite possible that both Luke and Paul meant, by baptism in the name of the Lord Jesus, Christian baptism as opposed to any other, and were not primarily concerned about the precise formula used at the time of that Christian baptism. Further *Didache* 7:1, a first century text, records baptism in the threefold name. This may not settle all the difficulties surrounding the matter in the New Testament, but there is no convincing argument against accepting those words in Matthew as the authoritative words of Jesus himself.[316]

Baptism reflects a dipping process; it means total immersion. It is the word used in the process of dying cloth. In the Bible, the writer of Revelation uses a form of the Greek verb *bapto* in this setting: "He is clad in a robe dyed (The NIV uses the word 'dipped') in blood, and the name by

---

[316] David Watson. I believe in the Church. London: Hodder and Stoughton, 1982, 1985. p. 228.

which he is called is the word of God."[317] A dyer, attempting to recolour his cloth would dip or immerse his cloth in the dyeing solution. The symbolism is interesting because it suggests the new status of the baptismal candidate whose "colours have changed!"

1. The Birthday of the Church

a. Belief and Baptism

The first occasion in which those coming to faith in Christ as Saviour and Messiah were baptized and taught followed ten days after Jesus' commission to his followers. The disciples were empowered by the incarnation of God the Holy Spirit as they assembled in a room. The incarnation in them of God's Spirit is what Jesus had instructed them to await.

> Do not leave Jerusalem, but wait for the gift my Father promised which you have heard me speak about. For John baptized with water, but in a few days you will be baptized with the Holy Spirit . . . But you will receive power when the Holy Spirit comes on you; and you will be my witnesses in Jerusalem, and in all Judea and Samaria, and to the ends of the earth.[318]

Jesus clearly underlined baptism as total immersion in God's full redemptive activity. Just as repentant persons demonstrate their burial of the old self and rising to the new life in Christ, so the new life is one which is a rebirth into spiritual existence fully governed by the presence and power

---

[317] Revelation 19:13.

[318] Acts 1:4, 5; Acts 1:8.

of God's Spirit.[319] In Jesus' own life, water and Spirit came together in the Jordan in his personal baptism.[320] It is a baptism which allows the Christian believer to say, "Jesus is Lord."[321] As Acts records, "Those who accepted his [Peter's] message were baptized."[322]

Jesus implied that it was faith in him as saving Lord and Messiah which was the key to entering the new community fellowship with him. The keys to God's kingdom were provided by the faith of those who made confession in Jesus.

> When Jesus came to the region of Caesarea Philippi, he asked his disciples, "Who do the people say the Son of Man is?" They replied, "Some say John the Baptist; others say Elijah; and still others, Jeremiah or one of the prophets." "But what about you" he asked, "Who do you say I am?" Simon Peter answered, "You are the Christ, the Son of the living God." Jesus replied, "Blessed are you, Simon son of Jonah, for this was not revealed to you by man but by my Father in heaven. And I tell you that you are Peter, and on this rock I will build my church, and the gates of Hades will not overcome it. I will give you the keys of the kingdom of heaven . . ."[323]

---

[319] Romans 6:1–14.

[320] John 1:32–34.

[321] 1 Corinthians 12:3, 12:8; Philippians 2:11;Philippians 3:8.

[322] Acts 2:41a.

[323] Matthew 16:13–19b.

The aforesaid text invites closer examination. Peter, in faith, responding to the revelation of the heavenly Father, had openly declared Jesus to be both Messiah (Christ) and the divine Son of God. Peter expressed what may have been in the minds of the other disciples but only Peter verbally responded in an act of overt faith.

Jesus declared that this was the rock on which his new community would be built. What did Jesus mean by "rock?" Was the rock Peter himself? Not likely, even though his name meant "rock" and he seemed to be the faith leader of the moment. Was the rock Christ? Possibly, but not likely! Would not Jesus have said, "I am the rock on which the church will be built" if that is what he meant? Was the rock the physical setting of the great grottoed rock face at Caesarea Philippi which was the centre of Pan worship and to which Jesus had taken his disciples to contrast himself with the decadent, pagan god of nature? Not likely!

The rock seems to have been the foundational act of faith by which Peter confessed Jesus as Messiah and God's Son. The key to God's kingdom, therefore, is not a person but an act of faith. This act of faith by Peter was echoed on the Day of Pentecost as wave after wave of men became believers in Jesus just as Peter had confessed at Caesarea Philippi. The church Jesus came to build, the new society in fellowship with God, was an organism based on the faith of those who overtly shared their belief through their initiating witness by immersion in the name of Jesus Christ.

b. Shavuot and the Spirit

Why did this event occur on *Shavuot*? In God's plan, one obvious reason was the reality that Pentecost brought such a variety of pilgrims to Jerusalem for the festival. When these pilgrims returned home with their new faith, they became immediate missionary witnesses to the communities of their origins about their new spiritual discovery. Even if they did not return home as believers, they still could not have been silent regarding the events on *Shavuot* in Jerusalem. They became automatic publicists of the Pentecost experience and in that way prepared the way for future missionary witnesses, such as Paul.

Moreover, *Shavuot* carried with it considerable symbolism. *Shavuot* was the festival of firstfruits. In that agricultural society God instructed his people[324] to give an offering to him as a reminder of the debt they owed God for the food and sustenance he provided for his people. That was the reason the pilgrims arrived in Jerusalem each year. Although they may have moved a great distance from their spiritual homeland, their ties to the graciousness of God were linked to Temple rituals. Moreover, God instructed them, "Three times a year all the men are to appear before the Sovereign LORD."[325] *Shavuot* was one of those three occasions.

Not all Jews were observant of the festivals nor of the rituals associated with them. However, a significant number of Jews followed the *Oral Torah* and subscribed to the requirements that were generally understood to be commandments. Oddly enough, some non-Jews obeyed the *Oral Torah* as part of their "seeking" process. How many Jews attended *Shavuot* each year is open to conjecture.

---

[324] Leviticus 23:10, 17; Exodus 23:19.

[325] Exodus 23:17.

Certainly, many pilgrim caravans made their way to Jerusalem from throughout the diaspora.[326]

> The full proselyte was bound to make the pilgrimage (cf Gal. 5:3 where Paul cites the Jewish regulations). But more than once we also come across so-called "God-fearers" at the festivals in Jerusalem: 'Now there were certain Greeks among those who went up to worship at the feast' (John 12:20): these were the uncircumcised "God-fearers," as was the treasurer of the Ethiopian Candace (Acts 8:28ff.). Josephus in BJ 6.427, mentions "any foreigners present for worship." In such cases the people were no doubt taking part of their own free will.[327]

How many people attended the festivals? Jeremias notes that the number suggested by Josephus to be three million pilgrims between 63-66 AD at Passover. Jeremias is doubtful. He thinks the number of pilgrims at a feast could vary from 65,000–125,000. Including the population in Palestine at the time, he asks if the figure of 180,000 is fixed too high?[328] If those numbers apply to Passover, they may also indicate the attendance at Pentecost.

Paul linked the gift of the Spirit of Pentecost to the celebration of *Shavuot*. He explained to Christians in Rome: "We ourselves, who have the firstfruits of the Spirit, groan inwardly as we wait eagerly for our adoption as sons, the

---

[326] Joachim Jeremias. Jerusalem in the Time of Jesus. p. 77.

[327] Ibid.

[328] Joachim Jeremias. op. cit. p. 84.

redemption of our bodies. For in this hope we were saved."[329]

The Holy Spirit was the symbol of God's promised redemption through Christ and God's gift to believers that one day they would be resurrected through their trust in Jesus' atonement on the cross. Not only did Paul make this clear to Roman believers, he further stressed it in his encyclical letter to the Ephesians.

> You also were included in Christ when you heard the word of truth, the gospel of your salvation. Having believed, you were marked in him with a seal, the promised Holy Spirit, who is a deposit guaranteeing our inheritance until the redemption of those who are God's possession – to the praise of his glory.[330]

Shavuot was at once the fulfilled promise of Jesus that he would send his Holy Spirit to believers,[331] and the assurance that trust in Jesus' atoning work on the cross, provided a new birth, eternal life and future resurrection for those putting their total faith in him. Paul further pointed to Jesus as the firstfruits of those others who, in trusting him for salvation, would eventually enjoy resurrection themselves.

> Christ has indeed been raised from the dead, the firstfruits of those who have fallen asleep. For since death came through a man, the resurrection of the dead comes through a man. For as in Adam all die, so in

---

[329] Romans 8:23.

[330] Ephesians 1:13, 14.

[331] John 16:7–15; Acts 1:5; Acts 1:8.

Christ all will be made alive. But each in his own turn: Christ, the firstfruits; then when he comes, all who belong to him.[332]

By virtue of the symbols of firstfruits through baptism in water and by God's Spirit, the believer's baptism represents burial to a former way of life and resurrection to a Spirit-incarnated existence in fellowship with God. This resurrected life is likewise a symbol of a future resurrection, as Paul put it, "when he comes [for] all who belong to him."

E. P. Sanders[333] has pointed to the basic fivefold Christian message held and delivered by Paul. The implications of them all can be expanded but the basics are simple bridges to the Spirit-filled life.

We see the emphasis of the Christian message: (1) God has sent his Son; (2) he was crucified, but for the benefit of humanity; (3) he was raised from the dead and exalted to heaven; (4) he would soon return, and those who belonged to him would live with him forever; (5) admonition to live by the highest ethical and moral standard: "May your soul and body be kept sound and blameless at the coming of the Lord Jesus Christ" (1 Thess. 5:23).

c. The Birthplace of the Church

The location of the events on the day of Pentecost (*Shavuot*) has few candidates. According to the text of Acts it was a location where Jews from the city and around the

---

[332] 1 Corinthians 15:20–23.

[333] E. P. Sanders. Paul. Oxford: Oxford University Press, p. 22.

Graeco-Roman world gathered to enter the Temple.[334] A house in which believers were gathered must have been nearby.[335] Those in the house – the Scriptures do not say how many – were "filled with the Holy Spirit."[336] Their enthusiasm must have spilled out into the nearby houses and streets, for the foreign pilgrims to Jerusalem heard the believers speaking each in his own language.

A pair of locations would provide opportunity for outsiders to be gathered *en masse*. One was the Royal Stoa or basilica which stood on the southern and southeastern rim of the Temple Mount. This site held the courts and provided public space for the merchants of international trade. Great deals were consummated within the precincts of the basilica as merchants from the Roman empire and spice traders from the east opted for Jerusalem as a significant trading centre. The Stoa was large. Its 300-metre length allowed hundreds of people within its open spaces.

Joachim Jeremias told of proselyte ritual washings that were held at the Pool of Siloam, a site where the priests always drew ceremonial water on the first seven days but not the last day of the Feast of Tabernacles (*Succoth*).[337] Jeremias wrote that "the baptism of proselytes in the Pool of Siloam in Jerusalem was not a rare occurrence. It is easy to imagine that Gentiles came to Jerusalem for their conversion

---

[334] Acts 2:5.

[335] Acts 2:2.

[336] Acts 2:4.

[337] George R. Beasley-Murray,. Word Bible Commentary: John Vol. 36 (second edition). pp. 113–115.

to Judaism."[338] Jeremias cited the Pool of Siloam as a location for proselyte immersions – and although it met the regulations for a *mikveh* in that it had running water – it likely was much too far from the location where Peter preached. Moreover, although it was much larger in Jesus' time period than today, it had insufficient room for 3,000 to be baptized. It remains an option for the baptisms of Pentecost, but an unlikely option. If the baptisms of Pentecost took place at Siloam, would not the biblical text have said so?

A more likely candidate for location was the Ophel. Ophel means "high place," or "uptown" in modern parlance. It was the upper town from David's original city after conquering the Jebusites. The Ophel was the male worshipper's gathering and preparation place for entering the Temple. Women entered the Temple precincts from a different portal. The Ophel was such a natural place for the events of Pentecost that the Scriptures may have assumed it did not need mentioning.

The prime reason for the pilgrims' visit to Jerusalem was spiritual, not economic – although the two motives often were intertwined in the ancient biblical world. Moreover, the pilgrims needed to spend some time at the Ophel in order to ritually prepare themselves for entry into the Temple precincts. Some would immerse themselves several times in the public *mikve'ot* to compensate fully with the requirement that every aspect of the body was totally immersed. Streams of pilgrims gathered at this preparatory spot. Some of the thousands of pilgrims on that *Shavuot* day likely used the

---

[338] Joachim Jeremias. Jerusalem in the Time of Jesus. Philadelphia: Fortress Press, 1969. p. 320.

private *mikve'ot* from the rooms they rented near the Ophel.[339]

The next criterion for location was the necessity of providing space for Peter to address the assembling multitudes. The Stoa may have had considerable space for hundreds of gathered people but it lacked the facilities for anyone addressing a large crowd. The Antonia, or Praetorium, on the northern edge of the Temple Mount had steps on which someone could address a sizable group of people. Paul did that as recorded in Acts 21:35. It was, however, an unlikely location for Peter to address the pilgrims who had come to Jerusalem for *Shavuot*.

The Ophel offered such a setting. It provided a platform from which Peter could address a significant crowd of people. If the numbers of pilgrims previously mentioned is correct – or approximately correct – even the minimum number of people listening to Peter preach may have numbered in the tens of thousands. Moreover, because it was stepped with staircases and progressively rising locations for *mikve'ot*, the Ophel allowed Peter to be both seen and heard by a maximum number of people.

One more important criterion for locating the birthing place of the church is that it required a venue for baptism. The Jordan River was two days' journey away and could not have been a candidate. Only the Ophel offered such a location. As previously noted, pilgrims were required to immerse themselves prior to entering the Temple grounds. The immersion vats already existed for that specific purpose. Peter, in response to those who asked what to do about the implications of Peter's address, invited those repenting of their sins and accepting Jesus as Saviour, Lord and Messiah,

---

[339] Meir Ben-Dov. op. cit. p. 153.

to be immersed in the name of Jesus Christ and receive God's gift to believers of the Holy Spirit.

What likely followed was that the apostles began baptizing believers in the name of Jesus and, in turn, the new believers began baptizing others as they openly declared their faith in Jesus the Christ. Perhaps the apostles started this process by baptizing one another – no other record is given of them being baptized in the name of Jesus. Finally, when *Shavuot* had concluded, 3,000 persons had accepted Peter's message and were baptized. Not only did the church find its life on that day in that place but it commissioned 3,000 believers to return to their communities throughout the Roman empire as witnesses of their new faith.

2.   Beyond Pentecost: Ongoing Believers' Baptisms

The ongoing connection of belief and baptism appears next in Acts 8.[340] Philip, the deacon,[341] was in Samaria "proclaiming" Christ. Healings of paralytics, disabled people and the "possessed" accompanied Philip's proclamation. An unnamed number of men and women were baptized "in the name of Jesus." Among them was a local magician, Simon Magus, who "believed and was baptized." The question is "what did he believe?"

Accounts of Philip's ministry and reports of healings and conversions reached the apostles in Jerusalem. In response, they delegated Peter and John to verify the authenticity of the reports. Peter and John's test of authenticity was to ask if the converts had received the Holy

---

[340] Acts 8:5–25.

[341] Acts 6:5.

Spirit. They discovered that they had only been baptized in the name of Jesus.[342] The two apostles then laid their hands on those who had been baptized and they received the Holy Spirit.

Simon Magus also wanted the Holy Spirit. Simon jealously thought he could pay for such a gift. Peter rebuffed him indicating that Simon's heart was wrong and that he needed to repent of this sin of trying to bribe God for a grace that is free. Simon did so and begged Peter to priest to God on his behalf. Peter and John departed, using their remaining time in "preaching the gospel in many Samaritan villages."[343]

The interval between baptism in the name of Jesus and receipt of the Holy Spirit raises an interesting question. On the Day of Pentecost, those who believed and were baptized in the name of Jesus received the Holy Spirit right away.

Not so in Samaria! The Bible offers no consistent answer to this issue. In some instances, for example, in Ephesus,[344] as here in Samaria, the act of laying on hands was associated with the reception of the Holy Spirit. Is it possible that the Jerusalem apostles, knowing the disposition of the animosity between Jews and Samaritans, wanted to authenticate that God's hand clearly was on the ministry of Philip to the Samaritans? Samaritans eschewed Jerusalem worship[345] and Jews forbad Samaritans from the Temple precincts. Part, but by no means all, of the enmity between

---

[342] Acts 8:16b.

[343] Acts 8:25.

[344] Acts 19:1 ff.

[345] John 4:20.

the two groups of Hebrews, resided in the difficulties Nehemiah had in rebuilding Jerusalem's walls upon the Jews' return from exile.[346]

Moreover, Jews regarded Samaritans as a "mixed" race, who settled in Assyria and returned without defining racial separation.[347] William E. Hull notes that the Samaritans resented the centralization of the sanctuary on Mount Zion "On one occasion . . . they retaliated by scattering human bones in the porticoes and throughout the Temple while the major Passover festival was in progress (Josephus, *Antiq.*, XVIII, 29–30.)."[348]

Did the Holy Spirit likewise ostracize Samaritans from enjoying the grace of God? They got their answer. Jesus' words about being witnesses in Samaria[349] had come to pass. God broke though the enmity between Jews and Samaritans by offering each an inclusive gospel. T. C. Smith writes:

We are safe in assuming that the reception of the Holy Spirit by the Samaritan converts was equally beneficial for the apostles. It proved to them that God was involved in the ministry among the Samaritans, and the church in Jerusalem must accept what God authenticated.?[350]

---

[346] Nehemiah 4:2.

[347] 2 Kings 17:24–41.

[348] William E. Hull. Broadman Bible Commentary: Luke–John. p. 249.

[349] Acts 1:8.

[350] T. C. Smith. Broadman Bible Commentary: Acts–1 Corinthians., p. 57.

The account in Acts which follows the telling of Philip's evangelism in Samaria relates Philip's witness to an individual near Gaza. In this account Acts relates how an "angel" (messenger) of the Lord instructed Philip to go to a desert road between Jerusalem and Gaza. The messenger did not tell Philip what to do but Philip knew instinctively to seize whatever opportunity presented itself. The opening turned out to be contact with an Ethiopian eunuch.

The Bible does not indicate that the eunuch was a Jew but he may have been. He had been to Jerusalem to worship. He could only worship from afar, however, because his sexual mutilation disallowed his presence at the Temple. The *Torah* clearly stated, "No one who has been emasculated by crushing or cutting may enter the assembly of the LORD."[351] Isaiah toned down that overt discrimination by citing the LORD's prophecy: "Let no foreigner who has bound himself to the LORD say, 'The LORD will surely exclude me from his people.' And let not any eunuch complain, 'I am only a dry tree.'"[352]

Perhaps the eunuch was confused by Isaiah. His interest certainly was piqued by reading Isaiah 53:7, 8, a passage which alluded to Jesus' atonement. Philip explained to him that Jesus had fulfilled all that Isaiah predicted. Passing by a body of water, the now-believing eunuch asked if he could be baptized and so he was. The man who was refused entry into the community of Israel was able to enter the new community of faith in Jesus Christ. This time, the Bible does not mention the receipt of the Holy Spirit as such. However, its inference that "when they came up out of the

---

[351] Deuteronomy 23:1.

[352] Isaiah 56:3.

water [implied immersion] the Spirit of the LORD suddenly took Philip away,"[353] suggests that the Spirit was part of the process. What else may interest a reader is that the baptism did not take place within the community of faith. Perhaps only the eunuch's carriage driver or attendant was present.

The Bible takes its readers next to the conversion of Saul, also known as Paul. In this account Paul was converted, received the Holy Spirit and then was baptized.[354] In a retelling of this story, Paul made no mention of the Holy Spirit but spoke only of his baptism and of the washing of his sins away, calling on his [Jesus'] name.[355] In the third version of his conversion Paul mentioned neither his baptism nor the Holy Spirit – probably because the occasion did not call for it.

Acts relates a further anecdote about baptism among the Gentiles in Caesarea Maritima. This took place in the house of Cornelius where Peter, barely having arrived from Joppa, explained Jesus' life, death and resurrection to those assembled. As Peter preached:

The Holy Spirit came on all who heard the message. The circumcised believers who had come with Peter were astonished that the gift of the Holy Spirit had been poured out even on the Gentiles . . . Then Peter said, "Can anyone keep these people from being baptized with water? They have received the Holy Spirit just as we

---

[353] Acts 8:30; See also 1 Kings 18:12 about "where the Spirit of the LORD may take you."

[354] Acts 9:17, 18.

[355] Acts 22:16.

have." So he ordered that they be baptized in the name of Jesus Christ.?[356]

In this foregoing report the Holy Spirit came to believers before they acknowledged their faith in Jesus as Messiah and Saviour. T. C. Smith suggests that this order of Spirit first and baptism afterward was not the norm of the Acts reports. "The departure from the normal order of events, which was faith, baptism and reception of the Holy Spirit, was an indication that God had inaugurated the acceptance" [of Gentiles into the new family of believers in Christ].[357]

Or was the order of things correct after all? Was not the Holy Spirit at work preparing the receptivity of Peter's message and is not faith also a gift from God's Spirit? Moreover, much interpretation relies on the meaning of "heard." In the prayer *Shema Yisrael* of the *Torah*[358], the word "hear" has several meanings. It means at once "listen," "understand" and "act upon."[359]

The *Shema* was and is recited by observant Jews in the evening and in the morning each day. Perhaps, and not implausibly, when Acts reported that Gentiles "heard" the message, the Gentiles may have "listened," "understood" and, in faith, "acted upon" Peter's enthusiastic declaration of the gospel.

---

[356] Acts 10:47, 48.

[357] T. C. Smith. op. cit. p. 70.

[358] Deuteronomy 6:4.

[359] John D. W. Watts. Broadman Bible Commentary, Vol. 2: Leviticus–Ruth, p. 212.

3. Household (*Oike*) Baptisms

Acts 16 reports two "household" or "*oike*" baptisms. In both instances no mention is made of the Holy Spirit. Mention is made, however, of faith reaction to Paul's declaration of Christ. In each instance, the conversions are within Gentile ambiences.

The first of these is the conversion of Lydia, a textile representative from the Lydian community of Thyatira. Lydia is described as "a worshipper of God."[360] Paul and his team entered Philippi and immediately sought a gathering of the synagogue to which they could join in prayer and offer their insights that Jesus, the Messiah, had come, had died and had risen from death.

Apparently too few Jewish males lived in that Roman colony, so a congregation of Jewish women and/or God worshippers gathered for public worship. They met at the riverside, an appropriate place because they could immerse themselves in a *mikveh* ritual before commencing their prayer activity. Paul and his companions knew instinctively ("Where we expected there to be a place of prayer")[361] that is where Jews would meet if they had no building in which to worship. They perhaps could have met in Lydia's house but her status as a woman and a non-Jew may have prohibited that.

Lydia was ripe for Paul's presentation of the gospel. "The Lord opened her heart to respond to Paul's

---

[360] Acts 16:14.

[361] Acts 16:13.

message."[362] Lydia and her entire household were baptized. Acts implies but does not categorically argue, that the entire household believed. The household likely included her staff, as possibly she had no family.

The second reported household baptism links belief of the household members with their baptisms. More likely, these were family members rather than servants. Their ages are not offered to the reader.

> He [the jailer] asked, "Sirs, what must I do to be saved?" They replied, "Believe in the Lord Jesus, and you will be saved – you and your household." Then they spoke the word of the Lord to him and all the others in his house . . . he and all his family were baptized . . . he was filled with joy because he had come to believe in God – he and his whole family.[363]

In these two household baptisms no mention is made of the Holy Spirit as such, but Acts does say that the Lord opened Lydia's heart to respond to Paul's presentation[364] and in the jailer's conversion we read that his heart was "filled" with joy,[365] indicating the presence of the Spirit in his life. It would seem wrong to argue that because the Holy Spirit was not mentioned precisely in those words that these conversions were not accompanied by the Spirit's presence and action. It likewise would seem wrong to infer that

---

[362] Acts 16:14.

[363] Acts 16:30–34.

[364] Acts 16:14.

[365] Acts 16:34.

incompetents, such as small children, were included in the household baptisms.

Where and when did this jailer's household baptisms take place? The text is unspecific about timing or location. To the reporter of Acts, it obviously was an incidental question. Nonetheless, the reader can be curious and ask for probable answers. David Edwards pondered the issue also.

> We do not know as much as we should like. There was no river in that prison, and we do not know how water was poured over the jailer and his family. That night it was all over in a matter of hours – but we do know what preparation was normally given to candidates. We are told that the jailer's household was were baptized, but we are not told whether this included children too young to understand or adults too sceptical to be converted there and then.[366]

Edwards' questions can partially be answered with alternative suggestions. First, baptism by pouring would not have made sense because immersion was the norm. Edwards' suggestion of pouring surely is an anachronism of much later ecclesiastical interpretation. Baptism meant immersion.

Secondly, a river did and does flow through Philippi. This writer has visited both the river and the traditional site of the jail in which Paul and Silas were imprisoned. J. R. Porter, professor emeritus of theology at the University of Exeter, England, describes this prison as "believed to be on

---

[366] David Edwards. <u>Good News in Acts</u>. Glasgow: Fontana Books (Collins) p. 86.

the same site as the cell in which Paul was detained."[367] The river and the jail are less than a kilometre apart. It is deep enough even in a drier season for someone to lie prone in the riverbed while water rushed over the person. Likely that is where Lydia was baptized. The prayer group Paul and his team happened upon, habitually met by the riverside. Surely it would have been the appropriate place for the jailer's family to be baptized!

Here is a possible alternative scenario. The earthquake which liberated Paul and Silas from their fetters occurred at midnight.[368] Perhaps that meant 12 o'clock – but not necessarily. Was that a Roman or Jewish description of the time? In the Gospels, Luke uses Jewish time to describe the death of Jesus.[369] Possibly, midnight is a generalization, meaning "in the middle of the night."

Whatever time was used to describe midnight, the consequence is that subsequent actions of Paul, Silas, the jailer, the treating of wounds, spiritual discussions, family awakening and joining in all of these, suggest early morning by the time any baptisms could take place.

Perhaps Paul and Silas proposed that a public location for the baptisms was appropriate, such as the river. Moreover, since Paul also demanded a public apology from the city magistrates for misjudging his citizenship, would he also not have required a public baptism of the converts, with the new Christians – Lydia and her household –

---

[367] J. R. Porter. The Illustrated Guide to the Bible. Toronto: Élan Press. 1995. p. 246.

[368] Acts 16:25.

[369] Luke 23:44. See also Summers, Ray. Commentary on Luke, p. 303.

sympathetically supporting them along the banks of the river? That explanation seems more plausible to this writer than does that of David Edwards.

4. Pauline and Petrine Baptismal Theology

In Acts and in the New Testament writings, Luke, Paul, and Peter lay down some clear baptismal theological principles. Baptism was seen as the norm of Christian initiation into Christ's family of faith. The book of Hebrews refers to instruction about baptisms as foundational to Christian faith and action. Hebrews suggests that baptism is so elementary a subject – just like repentance from sin, discussions about the resurrection and of judgment – that the readers should move on to more mature issues in the Christian faith.[370]

a. Baptism as Personal

One sees a clear teaching – shared by Paul, Aquila and Priscilla – about the theology of baptism as shown in the incidents related to Apollos at Ephesus.[371] In this episode reported in Acts, the three met Apollos, a very eloquent preacher who had become a disciple of John the Baptist. As Billy E. Simmons put it,

> Paul's encounter with the followers of John the Baptist indicated that Christianity had not completely succeeded in claiming all of those who had followed John during his ministry. These men apparently believed John's message that Jesus was the Messiah. But they seemed to

---

[370] Hebrews 6:2.

[371] Acts 18:25, 26; Acts 19:1–7.

have been unaware of all that Jesus did. They certainly were unaware of the continuing work of Christ through his Spirit. The outward signs of the Spirit's fulness forecast the significant work God was going to do in and around Ephesus."[372]

First, Acts reports that Aquila and Priscilla took Apollos aside "and explained to him the way of God more adequately."[373] Then Paul asked a pertinent question: "Did you receive the Holy Spirit when you believed?"[374] The King James Version translates that question as, "Have ye received the Holy Ghost since ye believed?" This writer prefers "when" over "since" as more consistent with other events related to the Holy Spirit.

Paul insisted that Apollos and the dozen followers of Apollos be immersed "in the name of Jesus." Paul reasoned that repentance alone is insufficient as a basis for Christian baptism. He also considers the previous "baptisms" of and by Apollos to be invalid. An important principle is at stake here. Baptism in and of itself has no saving efficacy. Paul has insisted that the candidate for baptism know Jesus experientially and personally claim Jesus not only as Messiah but trust him to be Saviour and Lord.

b. Baptism as Personal and Individual

This theological principle addresses a strange comment by Paul about proxy baptism. Paul used an abstruse

---

[372] Billy E. Simmons. <u>A Study Guide to Acts</u>. Nashville: The Sunday School Board of the Southern Baptist Convention, 1972. p. 98.

[373] Acts 18:26.

[374] Acts 19:2.

argument to claim that believers truly understood and expected a personal resurrection. In so doing he mentioned a custom among some believers who were baptized "for the dead."[375] In other words, some people in Corinth were baptized because they hoped their experiential belief would suffice for relatives or friends who had died not knowing the truth about Jesus and unbelieving in Jesus' messiahship or atonement.

Gerald L. Borchert commented:

Few texts in the New Testament have been the subject of a greater variety of interpretations than these verses (1 Cor. 15:29–32). Some think that there are nearly two hundred views concerning the baptism for the dead. Obviously here only a brief review is possible. Hans Lietzmann argues that proxy baptism may have at first been recognized by some and later rejected. He thinks that John Crysostom may be describing a similar Marcionite practice where a person emerges from below the bed of a dead person and answers questions put to the dead person. Luther rejects the proxy view and chooses the unlikely translation for *huper* of baptizing "over" dead bodies. Mathias Rissi suggests that the dead here died in some accident or epidemic, and baptism was employed by the survivors as a confessional proclamation of their faith. Barrett thinks that since Paul de-emphasises baptism at Corinth (1 Cor. 1:14–17), some Christians died without baptism, and the baptismal rite was performed for them by survivors. Conzelmann holds that such confessional interpretations are too contemporary and that the Corinthians were basically sacramentalists. Bruce is moved by Raeder's argument that some survivors sought baptism 'to be united with their departed Christian friends in the life to come.'

---

[375] 1 Corinthians 15:29.

The massive number of interpretations makes it clear that although the Corinthians probably understood Paul's passing reference, modern scholars cannot be certain of the Corinthian practice. That it is nowhere else discussed in the New Testament warns against regarding it as a tenet of Christian theology. Whatever it means, Paul would not accept any suggestion that a baptismal act on behalf of the dead could transform a dead believer into a believer. The text itself cannot be said either to affirm or to deny the practice. But what may be noted is that Paul uses the Corinthian practice to prove the futile nature of their denial of the resurrection.[376]

It would be easy to dismiss the idea of proxy baptism as bizarre except that Paul sometimes used arcane arguments to try to prove a point. For example, in his advice on marriage, Paul wrote to Corinth that "the unbelieving husband has been sanctified through his wife and the unbelieving wife has been sanctified through her believing husband. Otherwise your children would be unclean, but as it is, they are holy."[377]

On the other hand, Paul seems to undo that argument in his next letter to Corinth. This time, his advice seems contradictory to his previous position. "Do not be yoked together with unbelievers. For what do righteousness and wickedness have in common? Or what fellowship can light have with darkness? What harmony is there between Christ and Belial? What does a believer have in common with an unbeliever?"[378]

---

[376] Gerald L. Borchert. *The Resurrection*. Review and Expositor, Vol. LXXX, No. 3, Summer, 1983. p. 409.

[377] 1 Corinthians 7:14.

[378] 2 Corinthians 6:14, 15.

Paul likewise appears contradictory in his teaching about the women of Corinth. In one admonition, the apostle declares that "is disgraceful for a woman to speak in the church."[379] What does that mean? A reader cannot fully know. A little earlier in the same letter, Paul argued that "every woman who prays or prophesies with her head uncovered dishonours her head."[380] A reader must ask the question, "How can she prophesy without speaking? Or consider that in his letter to Rome, Paul sends his commendation to "our sister Phoebe." She is described in this letter as a *diakonos*, (translated variously as *deacon, helper, leader, officer, servant*) of the church in Cenchrea[381] (only ten miles from Corinth). Paul cites a basic principle to the Galatians, that gender exists no more in the Christian vocabulary. "You are all one in Christ Jesus."[382]

Paul did not always appear to be consistent. Ergo, Paul's comment on proxy baptism lacks the authority of full apostolic endorsement.

Likely the practice of proxy baptism was limited, unusual and ill-conceived. Elements of the argument surfaced in later centuries with the subsequent practice of paedo-baptism and more recently in the nineteenth century with the rise of the Church of the Latter Day Saints (Mormons). This writer concludes it was a faux baptism, an aberration of true Christian baptism and unworthy of further consideration.

---

[379] 1 Corinthians 14:35.

[380] 1 Corinthians 11:5.

[381] Romans 16:2.

[382] Galatians 3:28.

5. Baptism as Initiation into Christ, His Ministry and the Community of Christ

To Paul, baptism was symbolic of something else. He used the symbol of baptism to describe the passage of the Israelites through the Red (Reed) Sea into their pilgrimage toward the promised land. "Our forefathers were all under the cloud and passed through the sea. They were all baptized into Moses in the cloud and in the sea."[383] Of course the Israelites did not get wet[384] in "passing through the sea," so the statement on their collective immersion is strictly symbolic. Fred Fisher writes:

[Paul] interprets the experience of Israel as a type of Christian baptism. *All were baptized*: the emphasis is on the *all* . . . All had the same experience. *Baptized* means literally "to be immersed" in something. The textual evidence is about evenly divided between the middle voice (they had themselves baptized) and the passive voice (they were baptized). Since it is more likely that a copyist would change the middle voice to the passive voice because this was the common voice used in speaking of Christian baptism, the reading of the middle voice should be preferred. The effect of this reading is to emphasize the willingness of the Israelites to accept baptism. There could be some question concerning Paul's purpose to make this typical of baptism. The Greek word, in itself, speaks only of an immersion.

---

[383] 1 Corinthians 10:1, 2.

[384] Exodus 14:22.

However, it seems best to let the reference to Christian baptism stand.[385]

In some instances, therefore, "to be baptized' meant "to be overwhelmed." Jesus spoke of his baptism in that way. His baptism in the Jordan pointed toward his death on the cross. He asked his disciples if they could be baptized with his baptism but he did not mean the Jordan experience.[386] Jesus meant the cross. David Watson explored the various meanings of baptism, including being inundated:

> The verb *baptizo* was used in pre-Christian Greek to mean "plunge, sink, drown, drench, overwhelm." A person could be overwhelmed (lit. baptized) by debts, sorrow, calamity; or overcome (lit. baptized) by wine or sleep. Euripedes in the Orestes uses *bapto* when water is splashing into a ship, but *baptizo* when the ship is waterlogged or sinking.[387]

> Jesus later identified himself with sinners in the fullest and most profound sense possible when on the cross he "became sin" for us; and it is worth noting that on two occasions Jesus spoke about his coming death in terms of baptism: "I have a baptism to be baptized with." It was through his baptism of suffering on the cross, when he took upon himself the full consequences of our sin, that forgiveness was made possible. Moreover, that

---

[385] Fred Fisher, <u>Commentary on 1 & 2 Corinthians</u>. Waco: Word Books, 1975. pp. 153, 4.

[386] Luke 12:50; Mark 10:38, 39.

[387]David Watson. <u>I Believe in the Church. London</u>: Hodder and Stoughton.1978. 1982. p. 226.

forgiveness symbolized by water baptism, could only be received through repentance and faith.[388]

Paul downplayed his own role as a baptizer. He was primarily a preacher and teacher and his teaching seems mainly to be found in his writings to the churches. He did not deny the great commission of Jesus – to make disciples, baptizing and teaching them – but clearly the ministry of baptizing was not his forte.

> Were you baptized into the name of Paul? I am thankful that I did not baptize any of you except Crispus and Gaius, so no one can say that you were baptized into my name. (Yes, I also baptized the household of Stephanas; beyond that, I don't remember anyone else.) For Christ did not send me to baptize, but to preach the gospel."[389]

Peter also references baptism as both individual and communal.

> For Christ died for sins once for all, the righteous for the unrighteous, to bring you to God. He was put to death in the body but was made alive by the Spirit, through whom he also went and preached to the spirits in prison who disobeyed long ago when God waited patiently in the days of Noah while the ark was being built. In it only a few people were saved through water, and this water symbolizes baptism that now saves you also – not the removal of dirt from the body but the pledge of a good conscience toward God. It saves you by the resurrection of Jesus Christ, who has gone into heaven and is at

---

[388] David Watson. op. cit. pp. 227, 228.

[389] 1 Corinthians 1:13–17.

156

God's right hand – with angels, authorities and powers in submission to him.[390]

Some issues result from this writing of Peter. One is that Peter uses the same symbolism of baptism as Paul in referring to a "dry" baptism. Those in the ark, like the Israelites crossing the Red Sea, were saved from the waters of the flood. So this is an analogous reference to baptism and salvation. Translator J. B. Phillips commented:

> The waters of the Flood were to him [Noah] a prefiguring of the waters of baptism. Washing with water means far more than the cleansing of the body; it is the outward sign of a clean inner attitude towards God. This latter, which is no less a miracle, is made possible by the same power which raised Jesus from the dead and restored him to his position of power and authority in the timeless world of what we call, for want of a better word, "heaven."[391]

A second issue is the saving efficacy of baptism itself. Peter's phrase "this water symbolizes baptism that now saves you"[392] in no way suggests that the water itself has saving power. Baptism is *not* sacerdotal. What *does* save "us" is "our" (the believer's) faith/trust connection to the atoning work of Christ on the cross and his subsequent rising from death. Peter explains this clearly: "It saves you . . . by the resurrection of Jesus Christ."[393]

---

[390] 1 Peter 3:18–22.

[391] J. D. Phillips. Peter's Portrait of Jesus. p. 163.

[392] 1 Peter 3:21.

[393] Ibid.

Bo Reicke's insights should also be considered in this Petrine passage.

> When it is stated that baptism "now" saves the Christian believers, it is most natural to understand the time reference as part of an actual baptismal service. The expression itself need only mean that baptism is always a present reality in the life of the Christian, but such an indefinite, generalized interpretation does not do justice to the epistle. Here the believers, throughout the early chapters are treated as recently converted individuals. Furthermore, in the characterization of baptism which follows, emphasis centres upon a specific deed or event rather than on a persisting condition or state. We conclude, with reference to the first part of the epistle, that a baptismal ceremony is about to be celebrated, or has just taken place.[394]

The third issue is the collective and corporate salvation which those in Noah's ark experienced. They truly were a "fellowship of the saved" just as those perishing had become the "fellowship of the damned." This corporate identity is like that of the church, people "all in the same boat" as it were, who discovered the saving nature of God's grace. This mutual experience of grace gives those receiving it a kindred fellowship and new mutuality. That new "fellowship of the saved" is reflected in Peter's earlier words urging believers to become the "fellowship of the saving." "Finally, all of you, have unity of spirit, sympathy, love of the brethren, a tender heart and a humble mind. Do not return evil for evil

---

[394] Bo Reicke. The Anchor Bible: Vol. 37, The Epistles of James, Peter, and Jude. Garden City New York: Doubleday and Company, 1964, 1981, p. 114.

or reviling for reviling; but on the contrary bless, for to this you have been called, that you may obtain a blessing."[395]

Richard N. Longenecker, in his commentary on Galatians notes the importance of linking Christ to the entire transformed community by stating, "You are all sons of God."[396] "That 'all' (*pantes*) is meant to be emphatic is indicated not only by its position at the beginning of the sentence but also by the universality in vv. 27–28 and in Gentile Christians as 'Abraham's seed' in v. 29."[397] God's mercy shows incredulous breadth by enwrapping the entire gambit of the human family.

Paul, in writing to Corinth, Galatia, Ephesus and Rome, further connected baptism with the cross, Christ and the Christian community. In these communications he set down a basic universal proposition. Baptism connects all the fundamental strands of Christian faith – (1) initiation into Christ and the Christian life; (2) witness of one's spiritual metamorphosis from a former life to a new existence; (3) a drama illustrating the new birth, i.e., a witness to the death, burial and resurrection of Jesus Christ;(4) solidarity with the new society of the "saved"; and (5) a spiritual journey led by the Spirit of God.

a. Baptism – Initiation into Christ.

Paul emphasizes the concept that baptism in the name of Christ means initiation into Christ himself. C. H. Dodd points out that

---

[395] 1 Peter 3:8, 9.

[396] Galatians 3:26.

[397] Richard N. Longenecker. Word Biblical Commentary Vol. 41: Galatians. Waco: Word Books, 1990. p. 151.

The reference to baptism is of great value paedagogically . . . For here, in this sacrament, is something actually done – a step taken which can never be retraced. Before it a man was not a member of the Church, the people of God: now he is a member. If he should thereafter be unfaithful, that would not simply be a return to his former condition. Something has happened, something overt definable, with a setting in time and space, attested by witnesses. And behind that lies a similarly definite event in the inner life. He has grown into Christ. He is now in Christ."[398]

Moreover, a baptized person is also in the ministry of Christ.

Paul needed to remind Corinthian believers about being baptized into Christ. "Was Paul crucified for you? Were you baptized into the name of Paul?"[399] The meaning of "in" and "into" is exceedingly important. Immersion "in" or "into" the name of Christ meant absolute identity in full union with Christ. Note Mary Ann Getty:

The term "baptism" itself means immersion. This was literally signified in ancient ritual but is more symbolic in most Christian rites today. Paul's concern is clearly not with the rite itself or the formulas used in Baptism, but with the reality Baptism represents of immersion into Christ. This immersion into Christ's death and Resurrection is as irrevocable as the saving event itself. It is unthinkable to cross back over into the realm of death once one has been baptized into life with Christ.

---

[398] C. H. Dodd. The Epistle of Paul to the Romans.
Glasgow: Fontana Books (Collins), 1959. pp. 108-9

[399] 1 Corinthians 1:13.

Paul's Baptism theology is the basis of his mystical union-with-Christ description of the Christian life. Fully immersed into Christ, we have died with him (6:8). Our sinful inclinations were just as truly crucified and killed as Christ was (6:5–11). And now we are fully alive to God through the Resurrection. Just as Christ is.[400]

Baptism is the believer's unequivocal connection with Jesus Christ the Lord. Earl Palmer wrote:

That which dominates the whole passage, [Romans] 6:3–11, is the phrase "*into Christ Jesus.*" He [Paul] means that being a Christian involves our unique and individual ('all of us who have been . . .') relationship with Christ the one who died and was raised. Paul is teaching in this passage that baptism in the open acknowledgment and acceptance on the part of the Christian that the death and victory of Jesus is the event on my behalf. Baptism in this context is the Christian's answer to Romans 5:8, "God shows his love for us that while were yet sinners Christ died *for* us." By the sign of baptism the Christian, and the church along with him, gratefully replies, "The yes of faith in response to God's grace."[401]

Herschel Hobbs argues that baptism means immersion and that "immersion" is not a Baptist prejudice. Catholic comments run much the same as Protestants. He points out that all Greek lexicons describe the meaning of *baptizo* as

---

[400] Mary Ann Getty. Invitation to the New Testament: Epistles 1, Garden City New York: Image Books, 1982. pp. 184, 5.

[401] Earl F. Palmer. Salvation by Surprise. Waco: Word Books, 1975. p. 76.

immerse.[402] The word, as Hobbs explains, "is used in non-biblical Greek of a ship sinking. There was a time when one might need to dwell at length upon this matter, but no more. Scholarship is agreeing that the word means to immerse."[403]

Having stated that, Hobbs zeros in on the word "into."

> The key word in [Romans 6] verses 3–4 is "into" (*eis*, see Acts 2:38). Does it mean that in baptism the believer enters into Christ? No more so than "buried with him in baptism" means we enter into death (see v. 4). The preposition *eis* may be translated variously: into, unto, for, at (see Matthew 12:41), as the result of, with reference to. It seems that the last meaning applies here. Thus, "so many of us were baptized with reference to Christ Jesus, with reference to his death were baptized."[404]

b. Baptism – A Sign of One's Spiritual Metamorphosis

Baptism is a public testimony of a personal encounter with Christ through his Spirit. "Just as Christ was raised from the dead through the glory of the Father, we too may have a new life."[405] Hobbs interprets "the glory of the Father" as God's power reflected in the bodily resurrection of Christ.

The act of baptism illustrates what has happened to the new believer. He has renounced his former unspiritual life and has been born anew into the life of the risen Christ by

---

[402] Herschel H. Hobbs. Romans: A Verse by Verse Study. Waco: Word Books, 1977. p. 77.

[403] Ibid.

[404] Ibid.

[405] Romans 6:5.

the Spirit of God. He has come to know Christ, know in the sense of experiential discovery.[406] Hobbs further points out the importance of stressing both the death and resurrection of Jesus, as well as the death and resurrection of the baptismal candidate. "Christian baptism is immersion in water and emersion from water. Immersion alone is drowning. It depicts only a dying and burial. Emersion depicts a resurrection."[407]

That surely was what Paul meant in writing to Ephesus. Ephesians 2:1–22 discusses the death of those who renounced their unspirituality and found true, abundant life in Jesus.

> As for you, you were dead in your transgressions and sins in which you used to live . . . But because of his great love for us, God who is rich in mercy, made us alive with Christ even when we were dead in transgressions . . . And God raised us up with Christ."[408]

All this was for a purpose, of course. It was to illustrate God's power, grace, love, and mercy in the riches which he gives to his newly-born redeemed. Evidently, God wanted to show his "incomparable riches"[409] to future generations. The riches Paul wrote about are God's trophies, the men and women who have been bought at the cost of the cross. God invested his wealth in humanity and what has he to show for

---

[406] Herschel H. Hobbs. op. cit. p. 76.

[407] Ibid.

[408] Ephesians 2:1, 2, 4, 6.

[409] Ephesians 2:7.

his investment except those whose lives were made new by
the death and resurrection of Jesus?

c. Baptism – A Drama Illustrating the New Birth

Baptism is great theatre. Let no one think this
description of a deeply felt spiritual act diminishes its godly
intentions! Let "theatre" be a holy word in this instance.
Much of traditional Judaism provided great theatre whereby
great spiritual truths were taught. Examples of this are in the
story telling of the *Seder*,[410] the transfer of sin onto the
scapegoat,[411] the festivals of *Purim*,[412] *Succot(h)*[413] and
Shavuot,[414] the recitations of the *Shema*[415] or the washings of
Tevilah .[416]

Jewish ritual washing in the *mikveh* is likewise good
religious theatre. It differs from Christian baptism in a great
many ways. Undergoing ritual washing is deemed to be
meritorious for

the observant Jew. It is a physical act, not a symbolic
one. It is a private act, not a testimonial. It involves no

---

[410] Exodus 12:1 ff.

[411] Leviticus 16:10.

[412] Esther 9:20–28.

[413] Leviticus 23:33; Ezra 3:4; Nehemiah 8:14, 16.

[414] Exodus 22:29; 23:16; Nehemiah 10:35.

[415] Deuteronomy 6:4.

[416] See Dr. Yehoshua Cohen. The Laws of Tevilah.
Brooklyn NY: The Judaica Press, 1999.

special sense of repentance, rather, primarily an eagerness to be ritually correct. Nonetheless, it is good drama to impress on the individual involved in *Tevilah*, some basic teachings of the *Torah*. Consider its dramatic message: "When a person submerges himself in a *mikveh*, he momentarily enters the realm of the nonliving, so that when he emerges, he is like one reborn . . . to some degree this explains why a *mikveh* cannot be made in a vessel or tub, but must be built directly in the ground, for in a sense, the *mikveh* also represents the grave. When a person immerses, he is temporarily in a state of nonliving, and when he emerges, he is resurrected with a new status . . . The representation of the *mikveh* as both womb and grave is not a contradiction. Both are places of non-breathing and are end points of the cycle of life . . . when a person passes through one of these nodes (of the cycle of life), he attains a totally new status.[417]

Likewise, the Christian testimony of a public baptism illustrates the death, burial and resurrection of Jesus Christ. A baptismal experience in public is a dramatic presentation of gospel "basics."

When the candidate testifies that he is forever linked in trust to Jesus Christ the Lord as his Saviour, he, in effect, is "role playing" Jesus' words, "Into your hands I commit my Spirit."[418] At that moment the candidate has died to himself and turns his life over to God. Just as sympathizers and followers took Jesus' body down from the cross and laid it in

---

[417] Aryeh Kaplan. Waters of Eden. New York: National Conference of Synagogue Youth / Union of Orthodox Jewish Congregations of America. 1976, 1982, 1992, 1994, 1997. p. 14.

[418] Luke 23:46.

a tomb,[419] so the administrator of baptism, lays the candidate into the water, effectively burying him. The baptismal administrator likewise "role plays" the work of the Spirit. He lifts the "dead" candidate from the water, reflecting Paul's comment to the Romans, "The Spirit of him [God] . . . raised Jesus from the dead." [420] At once, the candidate "role plays" the risen Christ and the Christian life of the Spirit.

Baptism, then is very much an acted parable. It tells the gospel story in a compact drama. Each time it is played to an audience of believers or nonbelievers alike it reinforces the basic truth that Jesus Christ died for one's sins and rose again by the power of the Spirit of God. Karl Barth, in his commentary on Romans, indicates that one's faith is announced by our crucifixion with Christ. He points to seven dynamic words in Romans 6:8: "'If we died with Christ, we believe.' Dying with Christ is the vast negation beyond which by grace we stand."[421] In our witness to dying, we attest to our living faith in Christ.

d. Baptism – into Fellowship of the Saved

There is a further aspect to this baptismal candidature. The candidate is not baptized in seclusion. He or she witnesses to the reality that one is baptized into a new

---

[419] Luke 23:53; John 19:40;Mark 15:46.

[420] Romans 8:11

[421] Karl Barth. The Epistle to the Romans. Oxford: Oxford University Press, 1933. p. 201.

community. The new community is the commonwealth[422] of God, of which the church as the body of Christ[423] is a part.

Sharing in Christ's death, the new fellowship of the saved has likewise been privileged to share the Saviour's sorrows. Paul underscored this aspect of unity in Christ in addressing his Roman audience.

> The Spirit himself testifies that we are God's children. Now if we are children, then we are heirs – heirs of God and coheirs with Christ, if indeed we share in his sufferings in order that we may also share in his glory.[424]

Paul underlined this Christian mutuality when he attempted to draw the Judaizers into harmony with other converts in the area of Galatia. The Galatians – or an element among them – failed to see the reality that, in Christ, social, gender-sexual, economic, educational and employment differences dissipated when God, through Christ, created the newly "saved" individual. This implied not only a new mutuality among the believers but an accepted diversity among the unity. Thus, Gentiles did not have to become Jews in order to receive the grace of God or his Spirit. Yet Jews and Gentiles *together*, males and females *together*, bondservant and slave owner *together*, genteel aristocrat and unpolished foreign dock worker *together*, were new creations of God himself!

> You are all sons of God through faith in Christ Jesus, for all of you who were baptized into Christ clothed

---

[422] Ephesians 2:12; John 3:3.

[423] 1 Corinthians 10:16; Colossian 1:15–19.

[424] Romans 8:17.

yourselves with Christ. There is neither Jew nor Greek, slave nor free, male nor female, for you are all one in Christ Jesus. If you belong to Christ, then you are Abraham's seed and heirs according to the promise [God made to Abraham].[425]

Paul further stressed the importance of this unity of Jews and Gentiles into the new Israel by writing to Ephesians Christians: "This mystery is through the gospel, the Gentiles are heirs together with Israel, members together in one body, and sharers together in the promises of Christ Jesus."[426]

Make every effort to keep the unity of the Spirit through the bond of peace. There is one body and one Spirit – just as you were called to one hope when you were called – one Lord, one faith, one baptism; one God and Father of all, who is over all and through all and in all.[427]

In the aforementioned Galatian passage, Paul wrote about being "clothed with Christ." Clothing is also a metaphor, a dramatic idiom for the believer's appearance. The imagery also appears in the apostle's letter to Ephesus. Paul wrote there about putting off the "old self,"[428] e.g.,

---

[425] Galatians 3:26–29.

[426] Ephesians 3:6; see also Romans 3:29; Romans 4:16, 25; Romans 15: 5 ff.

[427] Ephesians 4:3–6.

[428] Ephesians 4:22.

"falsehood,"[429] and putting on the "new self"[430] since we have been "created to be like God in true righteousness and holiness."[431]

This may also have been a reference to the actual New Testament administration of baptism in which a candidate's clothes may have been discarded in the water, and a new robe worn for emergence from the place of baptism.[432] Its main meaning is to be solidly united with Christ so that those seeing a Christian will see him or her just as one sees Christ. Like the angels,[433] the new community would have the new garments fitting for the body of Christ.

e. Baptism – A Spiritual Journey Led by God's Spirit

"Buried with him through baptism into death . . . we too may have a new life."[434] The new life is the abundant life to which Jesus referred.[435] Jesus said, "Spirit gives birth to

---

[429] Ephesians 4:25.

[430] Ephesians 4:24.

[431] Ibid.

[432] Bo Reicke. op cit., p. 115; Longenecker, Richard N. op. cit., p. 154; John MacGorman. William. The Broadman Bible Commentary Vol 11: Galatians. Nashville: Broadman Press. 1971. p. 103.

[433] Acts 10:30.

[434] Romans 6:4.

[435] John 1:4; 10:10; 11:25; John 20:31.

spirit."[436] God's Spirit is the directing force which enables the newly baptized member of "the community of the saved" to find direction and service within God's kingdom. The Spirit helps us in our weakness, wrote Paul to Rome. "We do not know what we ought to pray for, but the Spirit himself intercedes for us . . . and he who searches our hearts knows the mind of the Spirit because the Spirit intercedes for the saints in accordance with God's will."[437]

The spiritual life cannot be advanced without the leadership of God's Spirit. Jesus said that without both "water and Spirit baptism" no one could enter God's kingdom. He knew disciples would more readily obey the water part of that insight but he knew they were less likely to allow the Spirit into their lives. That meant change – and change was and is in the Spirit's domain.[438] According to Jesus, his Spirit was life-giving,[439] kingdom-opening,[440]

---

[436] John 3:6.

[437] Romans 8:26, 27.

[438] John 3:5.

[439] John 7:17.

[440] John 3:5.

nourishing,[441] convicting,[442] empowering,[443] sanctifying,[444] and fruitful.[445]

Donald Kraybill has written about the reverse world of Christian versus non-spiritual belief. It is reversed to the materialistic concept of reality, that is. He notes:

> The community is essential as a corporate witness to God's love and grace . . . The Christian community is a profound witness to how God wills people to live and do business together. It's a demonstration of a new society of redeemed people.
> The community is also necessary to discern the real issues in modern life. An individual can easily be overwhelmed by the media blitz. The consumer demons of today come sugarcoated. The individual cannot always detect the depravity behind much of the rhetoric in modern life. The Holy Spirit in the community of faith helps God's people truly discern the times in which they live. Out of the corporate life the Spirit shapes the strategies for the involvement of Christ's disciples in the world. As the times and gifts are discerned, God's people are mobilized for significant ministries."[446]

---

[441] John 7:37, 38.

[442] John 16:8.

[443] Acts 1:8.

[444] John 17:17.

[445] John 15:5.

[446] Donald B. Kraybill. The Upside-Down Kingdom. Scottdale Pennsylvania: Herald Press. 1978. p. 306.

Christian pilgrimage begins at baptism and continues to the end of time under the Spirit's leadership. The Holy Spirit's presence at baptism means the continuance of Spirit leadership throughout life. In this journey by water and Spirit the believer will ultimately know the full import of Paul's words to Corinth: "Just as we have borne the likeness of the earthly man, so shall we bear the likeness of the man from heaven."[447]

---

[447] 1 Corinthians 15:49.

Summary

In this study we have examined what some might call the evolution of baptism. In a way it is an evolution, moving from the practice of Jewish ritual washing through to Christian baptism. In another way, Christian baptism is quite unlike Jewish ritual washing. "Evolution" would be an incorrect explanation in the relationship between baptism and ritual washing. Christian baptism is much more of a revolution than an evolution.

We have noted five steps in this revolutionary process. Traditional Judaism treated ritual washing by self-immersion as an important preparation for the worship of God. It was considered a preliminary step in the worship experience – indeed, a required one at the Temple in Jerusalem in the Herodian and New Testament periods.

The Qumran sect altered the concept of ritual immersion to mean more than a physical act to achieve righteousness as was the accepted idea in traditional Judaism. It was important for these Essenes to add a moral imperative to the physical act. Such acts of purification also required acts of confession and reconciliation. A fellow monk must also make peace with himself and anyone else in the community whom he has offended. Or if his problem is venal, he must also admit to that before taking his place in the *mikveh*.

Moreover, because the communal meal among the Qumranites was something of a substitute for the sacrificial cult activities in Jerusalem, each meal took on sacramental proportion and so preparatory immersion became mandatory.

With John the Baptist, ritual immersion crossed the line from Judaism into "Christian" territory and was now referred to as baptism. John, like the Essenes, operated from an eschatological bent, but his forward-looking stance involved the imminence of Messiah's arrival. The Essenes looked somewhat further ahead for their Teacher of Righteousness.

John's baptism was clearly both an opportunity for public repentance and a herald of Messiah's coming. A further signal in John's baptism was that John welcomed and invited Gentiles to receive the forgiveness of God. The Christian connection is that Jesus used this opportunity to welcome his herald's work and to signal his association with repentant sinners. The Spirit's presence at Jesus' baptism confirmed the Father's blessing and initiated Jesus' three-year ministry. His baptism likewise pointed forward to the cross and resurrection.

Following this work of John the Baptist, we learn from Jesus himself about the meaning of baptism. It is to be combined with the work of the Holy Spirit. Jesus' own baptism testified to this truth. Admission to God's kingdom needed more than repentance and more than ritual. Water must call to Spirit and Spirit to the water baptism.

Finally, we noted the first Christian *per se* baptism of believers at Pentecost. Baptism, explicit faith in Christ and presence of the Holy Spirit, were interconnected with each other and the believer. Moreover, this water and Spirit baptism in the name of Jesus meant a new mutuality in the "company of the saved," those who became part of Christ's body, the church.

Thus, Christians used the medium of baptism to express their unique faith in the death and resurrection of their Saviour, Jesus Christ and in the continuing presence of the Holy Spirit in their lives. This was indeed a novum, revolutionary, not evolutionary, even though Jewish ritual washing and Christian baptismal immersion have many similarities, i.e., total immersion, a sense of a new status, etc. It can be stated, however, that the beautiful Jewish tradition provided the wonderful imagery and the prompting to fully worship God in purity. For that, baptized believers can be forever grateful.

BIBLIOGRAPHY

Abbott, Walter M. (ed.) *The Documents of Vatican II.* New York: Guild Press, America Press, Association Press, 1966.

Abegg, Martin Jr., Flint, Peter, and Ulrich, Eugene. *The Dead Sea Scrolls Bible.* New York: Harper Collins, 1999.

Aland, Kurt. *Did The Early Church Baptize Infants?*, trans. G. R. Beasley-Murray. London: SCM, 1963.

Aldwinckle, Russell F., *Of Water and the Spirit: A Baptist View of Church Membership.* Brantford ON: Baptist Federation of Canada, 1964.

Alexandri, A. *Kos: Hippocrates' Island.* Athens: Sotiri Toumbi, 198?

Ariel, David S., *Spiritual Judaism*, New York: Hyperion, 1998.

Avigad, Nahman. *Discovering Jerusalem.* Israel: "Shikmona" Publishing Company, 1980.

_____. *The Herodian Quarter in Jerusalem*: Wohl Archaeological Museum. Jerusalem: Keter Publishing House, 1991.

Avi-Yonah, M. *Pictorial Guide to the Model of Ancient Jerusalem.* Jerusalem: Holy Land Corp., 197?.

Badia, Leonard F., *Qumran Baptism and John the Baptist's Baptism.* Lanham MD: University Press of America, 1980.

Barclay, William. *The Gospel of John Vol. 1.* Edinburgh: The Saint Andrew Press, 1955, 1973.

Barnes, William Wright. *The Southern Baptist Convention.* Nashville: Broadman Press. 1954.

Barth, Karl. *The Teaching of the Church Regarding Baptism*, trans. E. A. Payne. London: 1948.

_____. *Church Dogmatics IV The Doctrine of Reconciliation, Fragment.* Edinburgh: T & T. Clark, 1969.

Barkay, Gabriel. *Ketef Hinnom: A Treasure Facing Jerusalem's Walls.* Jerusalem: The Israel Museum, 1986.

Bassett, T. M. *The Welsh Baptists.* Swansea: Ilston House, 1977.

Beasley-Murray, George R. *Baptism in the New Testament.* London: Macmillan, 1962; Grand Rapids: Eerdmans, 1973.

_____. *Baptism Today and Tomorrow.* London: Macmillan, 1966.

_____. *Jesus and the Kingdom of God.* Grand Rapids: Eerdmans / Exeter UK: The Paternoster Press, 1986.

_____. *Word Bible Commentary, Vol 36: John.* Waco: Word Books, 1987.

_____. *Word Bible Commentary, Vol 36: John.* (Second Edition). Waco: Word Books, 1999.

Ben-Dov, Meir. *In the Shadow of the Temple.* Jerusalem: Keter Publishing House, 1985.

_____., ed. *Jerusalem Revealed.* Jerusalem: "Shikmona Publishing Company, 1975.

_____. *Herod's Mighty Temple Mount*, Biblical Archaeology Review Vol. XII, No. 6, November / December 1986, pp. 40–49.

Bishko, Herbert. *This Is Jerusalem*. Tel Aviv: Heritage Publishing Ltd., 1980.

Bonhoeffer, Dietrich. *The Cost of Discipleship*. London: SCM Press, 1937, 1959.

Brackney, William H. (ed.). *Bridging Cultures and Hemispheres*. Macon Ga: Smyth & Helwys, 1997.

_____. (ed). *The Believers Church: A Voluntary Church*. Pandora Press / Herald Press, 1996.

Bryan, F. C. ed. *Concerning Believers Baptism*. London: Kingsgate Press, 1943.

Bright, John. *A History of Israel*. London: SCM Press Ltd., 1959, 1972 (revised) 1979.

Buber, Martin. *Tales of the Hasidim*. New York: Schocken Books, 1947, 1975, 1991.

Burrows, Millar, *The Dead Sea Scrolls*. New York: The Viking Press, 1955, 1957.

Carr, Warren. *Baptism: Conscience and Clue for the Church*. New York: Holt, Rinehart and Winston, 1963.

Calvin, Jean. (McNeill John T., ed.; Battles, Ford Lewis, trans.). *Calvin: Institutes of the Christian Religion, The Library of Christian Classics Volume XXI*. London: SCM Press Ltd., 1961.

Champion, L. G. *Baptists and Unity*. London: A. R. Mowbray & Co., 1962.

Charif, Ruth and Raz, Simcha (eds.). *Jerusalem The Eternal Bond.* Tel Aviv: Don Publishing House, 1977.

Charlesworth, James H. (ed.). *Jesus and the Dead Sea Scrolls.* New York: Doubleday, 1992, 1995.

Clifford, Paul Rowntree. *The Christian Life.* London: The Carey Kingsgate Press, 1954, 1958.

Cohen, Yehoshua. *The Laws of Tevilah.* New York: Judaica Press, 1999.

Cohen, Abraham. *Everyman's Talmud.* New York: Schocken Books, 1949, 1975, 1995.

Cullmann, Oscar. *Baptism in the New Testament*, trans. J. K. S. Reid. London: SCM; Chicago, Regnery, 1950.

Danby, Herbert. *The Code of Maimonides. Book Ten: The Book of Cleanness.* New Haven: Yale University Press, London: Oxford University Press, 1954.

Dehan, Emmanuel. *The Chagall Windows: Symbols of the Twelve Tribes of Israel.* Tel Aviv: Emmanuel Dehan Publishing, 1979.

de Lange, Nicholas. *Judaism.* Oxford: Oxford University Press, 1986.

Demsky, Aaron. *When the Priests Trumpeted the Onset of the Sabbath.* Biblical Archaeology Review. Vol. XII, No. 6, November / December 1986, pp. 50–52.

Dosick, Wayne. *Living Judaism.* New York: HarperCollins, 1995.

Dimont, Max I. *Jews, God and History.* New York: Signet Books, 1962.

Earl, Ralph. *The Gospel of Mark: Proclaiming the New Testament.* Grand Rapids MI: Baker Book House. 1961.

Eliyahu, Harav Mordechai. *The Paths of Purity: The Laws of Niddah and Family Purity.* New York: American Friends of Sucath David Inc., 1986.

Eshel, Hanan. *The Pools of Sepphoris: They're Not Ritual Baths. Biblical Archaeology Review*, Vol. 26. No. 4, July / August 2000, p. 42.

Estep, William R. *Renaissance & Reformation.* Grand Rapids MI: William B. Eerdmans Publishing Company, 1986.

Fenton, J. C. *The Gospel of Saint Matthew.* London: Penguin Books, 1963, 1973.

Fitzmyer, Joseph H. *The Anchor Bible, Vol 28: The Gospel According to Luke I–IX.* Garden City NY: Doubleday & Co, 1981.

Flemmington, W. F. *The New Testament Doctrine of Baptism.* London: SPCK, 1948.

Forst, Rabbi Binyomin. *The Laws of Niddah.* Brooklyn NY: Mesorah Publications Ltd., 1997.

Gavin, F., *The Jewish Antecedents of the Christian Sacraments.* London: 1928.

Grafman, Ravi. *The Israel Museum Guide.* Jerusalem: The Israel Museum, 1983.

Gilbert, Martin. *Jerusalem Illustrated History Atlas.* New York: Macmillan Publishing Inc., 1977.

Gilmour, G. P. *The Memoirs Called Gospels*. Toronto: Clarke, Irwin & Company, 1959.

Gonen, Rivka. *Visualizing First Temple Jerusalem. Biblical Archaeology Review*, Vol. XV, No. 3, May / June 1989, pp. 52–55.

Greenslade, S. L. (translator and editor). *Early Latin Theology Volume V*. London: SCM Press Ltd., 1956.

Guiladi, Yael. *One Jerusalem*. Jerusalem: Keter Publishing House, 1979.

Hobbs, Herschel H. *The Gospel of Matthew: Proclaiming the New Testament*. Grand Rapids MI: Baker Book House, 1961.
_____.*The Baptist Faith and Message*. Nashville: Convention Press, 1971, 1987.

_____. *The Gospel of John: Invitation to Life*. Nashville: Convention Press, 1988.

Iakovidis, S. E. *Mycenae-Epidaurus*. Athens: Ekdotike Athenon S. A., 1982.

Ivison, Stuart and Rosser, Fred. *The Baptists in Upper and Lower Canada before 1820*. Toronto: University of Toronto Press. 1956.

Jeremias, Joachim. *Infant Baptism in the First Four Centuries*, trans. D. Cairns. London:SCM, 1960.

_____. *Jerusalem in the Time of Jesus*. Philadelphia: Fortress Press, 1969.

_____. *The Origins of Infant Baptism*. A Further Study in Reply to Kurt Aland. London: SCM, 1963.

Jocz, J. *The Spiritual History of Israel*. London: Eyre & Spottiswoode, 1961.

Jones, William H. *What Canadian Baptists Believe*. Toronto: ChiRho Communications, (revised) 1998.

Kahana, Kalman, trans. Oschry, Leonard. *Daughter of Israel: Laws of Family Purity*. Jerusalem: Feldham Publishers, 1970, 1973, 1995.

Kaplan, Aryeh. *Waters of Eden*: *The Mystery of the Mikvah*. New York: NCSY / Orthodox Union, 1982, 1988, 1992, 1994, 1997.

Kelso, James L. *An Archaeologist Looks at the Gospels*. Waco: Word Books, 1969, 1972, 1975.

Kenyon, Kathleen. *The Bible & Recent Archaeology*. London: The British Museum Publications, 1978, 1979, 1985, 1986.
_____. *Digging Up Jerusalem*. London and Tonbridge: Ernest Benn Limited, 1974.

Kochav, Sarah. *Mount of Olives, Gethsemane, Bethany*. Jerusalem: Yad Ben-Zvi Press, 1999.

Kraus, C. Norman. *Evangelicalism and Anabaptism*. Kitchener ON: Herald Press, 1979.

Landay, Jerry M. *Silent Cities, Sacred Stones*. New York: The McCall Publishing Company, 1971.

Latourette, Kenneth Scott. *A History of Christianity*. New York: Harper and Brothers Publishers, 1953.

Lazareth, William H., *Growing Together in Baptism, Eucharist and Ministry*: *A Study Guide* (Faith and Order Paper 114). Geneva: World Council of Churches, 1982.

_____. *Baptism, Eucharist and Ministry* (Faith and Order Paper 111). Geneva: World Council of Churches, 1982.

Lea, Thomas D. "Exegesis of Crucial Tests in John," *Southwestern Journal of Theology*. Vol. 31, Fall 1988 No. 1. Fort Worth: Southwestern Baptist Seminary.

Leavell, Roland Q. *Studies in Matthew: The King and the Kingdom*. Nashville: Convention Press, 1962.

Lerner, Michael. *Jewish Renewal*. New York: HarperCollins, 1995

Logiadou-Platonos, S. and Marinatos, Nanno, Crete. Athens: D. & I. Mathioulakis, 1986.

Lumpkin, William L. *A History of Immersion*. Nashville: Broadman Press, 1962.
MacBeath, John. *The Face of Christ*. Edinburgh: Marshall, Morgan & Scott, LTD., 1954.

Mare, W. Harold. *The Archaeology of the Jerusalem Area*. Grand Rapids: Baker Book House, 1987.

Marsh, Herbert G. *The Origin and Significance of New Testament Baptism*. Manchester: Manchester University Press, 1941.

Mazar, Eilat. *Excavations in the South of the Temple Mount: The Ophel of Biblical Jerusalem*. Jerusalem: Institute of Archaeology, Hebrew University of Jerusalem, 1989.

_____. "Royal Gateway to Ancient Jerusalem Uncovered." *Biblical Archaeology Review*, Vol. XV, No. 3, May / June 1989, pp. 38–51.

McCall, Duke ed. *Review and Expositor Vol LXV, No. 1 Winter 1968: Baptists and Baptism.* Louisville KY: Faculty of Southern Baptist Seminary, 1968.

Meuller, William A. *A History of The Southern Baptist Theological Seminary.* Nashville: Broadman Press, 1959.

Meyers, Eric M. "The Pools of Sepphoris: Yes, They Are." Biblical Archaelogical Review. Vol. 26, No. 4, July / August 2000. p. 46.

Montague, George T. *Mark: Good News for Hard Times.* Ann Arbor MI: Servant Books, 1981.

Moody, Dale. *Baptism For Christian Unity.* Philadelphia: Westminster, 1967.

Murphy-O'Connor, Jerome. *Oxford Archaeological Guides: The Holy Land. Oxford.* Oxford University Press, 1998.

Nineham, D. E. *The Gospel of Saint Mark.* Harmondsworth England: Penguin Books Ltd., 1963, 1973.

Nun, Mendel. *The Sea of Galilee and Its Fishermen in the New Testament.* Jerusalem. Kibbutz Ein Gev: Tourist Department and Kinnereth Sailing Co., 1989.

Oesterley, W. O. E., *A History of Israel Vol. II.* Oxford: Clarendon Press, 1934, 1939, 1945, 1948, 1951.

Papadakis, Theodore. *Epidauros: The Sanctuary of Asclepios.* Athens: Meletzis & Papadakis / Munich and Zurich: Schnell & Steiner, 1978.

Petrakos, Basil. *Delphi.* Athens: Clio Editions, 1977.

Polhill, John B. "The Revelation of True Life." *Review and Expositor*. Louisville: Southern Baptist Seminary, Vol. 85, No. 3, Summer 1988.

Reich, Ronny. Miqwa'ot (Jewish Ritual Baths) in Eretz-Israelin the Second Temple and Talmud Periods. Ph.D. dissertation, Hebrew University, Jerusalem, 1990.

Renfree, Harry A. *Heritage and Horizon: The Baptist Story in Canada*. Mississauga ON: Canadian Baptist Federation, 1988.

Reznick, Rabbi Leibel. *The Holy Temple Revisited*. Northvale New Jersey, London: Jason Aronson Inc.,1993.

Ritmeyer, Kathleen and Ritmeyer, Leen. "Reconstructing Herod's Temple Mount in Jerusalem." *Biblical Archaeology Review*, Vol. XV No. 6, November / December 1989, pp. 23–42.

Ritmeyer, Kathleen and Ritmeyer, Leen. "Reconstructing the Triple Gate." *Biblical Archaeology Review*, Vol. XV, No. 6, November / December 1989, pp. 49–53.

Ritmeyer, Leen. "Quarrying and Transporting Stones for Herod's Temple Mount." *Biblical Archaeology Review*. Vol. XV. No. 6, November / December 1989. pp. 46–48.
Ritmeyer, Kathleen. *A Pilgrim's Story. Biblical Archaeology Review*, Vol. XV, No. 6, November / December 1989, pp. 43–45.

Rosenberg, Stuart E., *To Understand Jews*. Toronto: PaperJacks, 1972.

_____. *The Real Jewish World*. Toronto: Clark Irwin, 1984.

Sanders, E. P. *Paul*. Oxford: Oxford University Press, 1991.

Schnackenburg, Rudolf. *Baptism in the Thought of St. Paul*: A Study in Pauline Theology, trans. G. R. Beasley-Murray. Oxford: Blackwell; New York: Herder & Herder, 1964.

Senior, Donald. *Invitation to Matthew*. Garden City NY: Image Books, 1977.

Shanks, Hershel. *The City of David: A Guide to Biblical Jerusalem*. Washington DC: The Biblical Archaeology Society, 1973, 1975.

Shanks, Hershel. "Excavating in the Shadow of the Temple Mount." *Biblical Archaeology Review*, Vol. XII No. 6., Washington DC, November / December 1986, pp 20–38.

_____.(editor). *Christianity and Rabbinic Judaism*. Washington DC: Biblical Archaeological Society, 1992.

_____. *Jerusalem – An Archaeological Biography*. New York: Random House. 1995.

Simon, Marcel (trans. by James H. Farley). *Jewish Sects at the Time of Jesus*. Philadelphia: Fortress Press, 1966.

Sirkis, R., *Bible Lands Museum Jerusalem: Guide to the Collection*. Jerusalem: R. Sirkus Publishers Ltd., 1992.

Strege, Merle D. (ed). *Baptism & Church: A Believers' Church Vision*. Grand Rapids MI: Sagamore Books, 1986.

Stone, Michael E. *Jewish Writings of the Second Temple Period*. Philadelphia: Van Gorcum, Assen Fortress Press, 1984.

Sullivan, James L. *John's Witness to Jesus*. Nashville: Convention Press. 1965.

Summers, Ray. *Commentary on Luke*. Waco TX: Word Books, 1972.

Schwartz, Hans. *The Christian Church*. Minneapolis: The Augsburg Publishing House, 1982.

Taylor, T. M., "The Beginnings of Jewish Proselyte Baptism," *New Testament Studies 2*, (1956).

Tendler, Harav Moshe David. *Pardes Rimonim: A Manuel for the Jewish Family*. Hoboken NJ: Ktav Publishing House Inc., 1988.

Torrance, Thomas F. "Proselyte Baptism," *New Testament Studies 1*, (1954).

_____. "The Origins of Baptism," *Scottish Journal of Theology 11* (1958).

Vermes, Geza. *The Dead Sea Scrolls in English*. Harmondsworth UK: Penguin Books Ltd., 1975.

_____. "Baptism and Jewish Exegesis, New Light from Ancient Sources," *New Testament Studies 4* (1958).

Walker, Williston. *A History of the Christian Church*. New York: Charles Scribner's Sons, 1959.

Walton, Robert C. *The Gathered Community*. London: Carey Press, 1846.
Watson, David. *I Believe in the Church*. London: Hodder and Stoughton, 1978.

Watts, Ronald F. *The Ordinances and Ministry of the Church: A Baptist View*. Toronto: Canadian Baptist Federation, 1986.

Whale, J. S. *Christian Doctrine*. Fontana Books / Collins, 1963.

Willimon, William H. *Remember Who You Are: Baptism, A Model for Christian Life*. Nashville: The Upper Room, 1980.

White, R. E. O. *The Biblical Doctrine of Initiation: A Theology of Baptism and Evangelism*. London: Hoder & Stoughton; Grand Rapids: Eerdmans, 1960.

Wood, Darryl. "The Logos Concept in the Prologue to the Gospel according to John." The Theological Educator. New Orleans: *New Orleans Baptist Theological Seminary*, No. 38, Fall 1988.

Yadin, Yigael. *Masada: Herod's Fortress and the Zealot's Last Stand*. Great Britain: George Weidenfeld & Nicholson Limited, 1966, 1984.

_____., ed. *Jerusalem Revealed*. Jerusalem: "Shikmona" Publishing company, 1975.

_____. *The Temple Scroll*. London: Weidenfeld and Nicolson. 1985.

Yancey, Philip. *The Jesus I Never Knew*. Grand Rapids MI: Zondervan Publishing House, 1995.

Zeitlin, Irving M. *Ancient Judaism*. Cambridge: Polity Press, 1984.

Zeitlin, Solomon. "A Note on Baptism for Proselytes," *Journal of Biblical Literature 52* (1933).

Major Ecclesiastical Reports

Church of Scotland Publications:
Interim Reports of the Special Commission on Baptism.
Edinburgh, 1955, 1956, 1958, 1959.

Draft of Interim Report 1956, Containing Detailed Reference Material Not Included in the Printed Report to the General Assembly (prepared by T. F. Torrence). Edinburgh, 1956

The Biblical Doctrine of Baptism: A Study Document Issued by the Special Commission on Baptism of the Church of Scotland. Edinburgh. Saint Andrew Press, 1960.

World Council of Churches Publications:
One Lord, One Baptism. London: SCM, 1960.

Baptism Eucharist, Ministry. Geneva: World Council of Churches, 1982.

Popular Periodicals

Agence France-Presse News Service. "Pilgrims Flock to Site of Christ's Baptism in Jordan." *National Post*, p. A16, 08 January 2000.

Albrecht-Weinberger, Karl. "Sephoris Synagogue Mosaic." *Newsletter* of the Jewish Museum of the City of Vienna. Vol. 23 Autumn '99.

Bernhard, Sandra. "Soul of Safed." Condé Nast *Traveler*, Sept. 1999, pp. 190–195.

Contenta, Sandro. "Fired Israeli Chef Fights a Secular War." *Toronto Star*, 02 October 1999, p. A27.

_____. "Was Jesus Baptized in Israel or Jordan?" *Toronto Star*, 27 November 1999. p. A18.
Csillag, Ron. "Holy Waters." *National Post,* 06 April 1999. P. B5.

Edmunds, E. *John Miles and the Ilston Baptists*. Aberdare, Wales: The Electric Press. Pamphlet published for the Unveiling Ceremony at Ilston, 1927.

Gibson, David, "I Think It's Disgusting: Will a $4 million Purification bath for Women Catch ON?" *The National Post*, 31January 2000, p. D4.

Growe, Sarah Jane, "Mikveh a Purifying Bath for Jews." *Toronto Star*, 06 September 1985., p. D2.

Hamilton, Masha. "'No Lights, No Bath, No Work Mark Ultra-Orthodox Sabbaths." *Toronto Star*, 07 November 1987.

Jiménez, Marina. "Muddying the Waters." *National Post*, p. A13, 03 January 2000.

Lichtblau, Dorothy. "Jewish Ritual Bath Being Clothed in Feminist Robes." *Toronto Star*. 19 June 1999.

Martin, Rev. Msgr. Paul. "What Was That Word?" *Sunday Bulletin*, Mission San Juan Capistrano, 19 January 1997.

_____. "Guidelines for Sponsors to a Baptism." *Sunday Bulletin*, Mission San Juan Capistrano, 25 January 1998.

McAteer, Michael. "How Jewish Is Christianity?" *Toronto Star*, 11 December 1999, p. N24.

Nicholas, Henry. *The Story of John Miles and Ilston*. Swansea: Ilston Press. 1949. Pamphlet published for the Welsh Baptist Ter-Centenary Celebrations, 1949.

Price, George Vernon. *Rhûal Baptistery. Restoration Souvenir*. Wrexham Wales: Publisher unknown. 1931.

Spurgeon, C. H., *Baptismal Regeneration* and *Children Brought to Christ–Not to the Font*. Metropolitan Tabernacle Pulpit, Sermons from Spurgeon During the Year 1864. Vol. X, Pasedena Texas: Pilgrim Publications, 1975.

Television

Paradox: Born King, A Television Production of CTV Toronto's Religious Advisory Committee, Toronto. Bill Burrows, producer, 1982.

www.ingramcontent.com/pod-product-compliance
Lightning Source LLC
Chambersburg PA
CBHW070409090426
42733CB00009B/1593